In the realm of ideas, to you: this record of patient research and genuine experiment according to experience, faithful to the nature of whatever was being done.

FRANK LLOYD WRIGHT, *Sixty Years of Living Architecture,* 1951

# FRANK LLOYD WRIGHT IN THE REALM OF IDEAS

EDITED BY BRUCE BROOKS PFEIFFER
AND GERALD NORDLAND

SOUTHERN ILLINOIS UNIVERSITY PRESS

CARBONDALE AND EDWARDSVILLE

*Frank Lloyd Wright at the Guggenheim Museum*

EXHIBITION ITINERARY

LTV Center Pavilion, Dallas Museum of Art, Dallas, Texas
*January–March 1988*

National Museum of American History (Smithsonian Institution),
Washington, D.C.
*July–September 1988*

Center for the Fine Arts, Miami, Florida
*December 1988–March 1989*

Museum of Science and Industry, Chicago, Illinois
*June–September 1989*

Scottsdale Center for the Arts, Scottsdale, Arizona
*January–March 1990*

San Diego Museum of Art, San Diego, California
*June–August 1990*

The exhibition Frank Lloyd Wright In the Realm of Ideas is organized and circulated by the Scottsdale Arts Center Association and the Frank Lloyd Wright Foundation.

The exhibition and its tour have been made possible by the generous support of Whirlpool Corporation and Kohler Co.

The City of Scottsdale has provided funding for the construction of the Usonian Automatic House.

Printed in Japan

Edited and Designed by Joyce Kachergis Book Design and Production, Bynum, North Carolina

00   99   98   97         13   12   11   10

LIBRARY OF CONGRESS CATALOGING-IN-PUBLICATION DATA

Frank Lloyd Wright in the realm of ideas.

"Exhibition itinerary: LTV Center Pavilion, Dallas Museum of Art, Dallas, Texas, January–March 1988; National Museum of American History (Smithsonian Institution), Washington, D.C., July–September 1988; Center for the Fine Arts, Miami, Florida, December 1988–March 1989; Museum of Science and Industry, Chicago, Illinois, June–September 1989; Scottsdale Center for the Arts, Scottsdale, Arizona, January–March 1990; San Diego Museum of Art, June–August 1990. The exhibition was organized by the Scottsdale Arts Center Association"—T.p. verso.
Bibliography: p.
1. Wright, Frank Lloyd, 1867–1959—Themes, motives—Exhibitions. 2. Architecture—United States—Themes, motives—Exhibitions. 3. Architecture, Modern—20th century—United States—Themes, motives—Exhibitions. I. Pfeiffer, Bruce Brooks. II. Nordland, Gerald. III. Dallas Museum of Art. IV. Scottsdale Arts Center Association.
NA737.W7 A4   1988        720'.92'4        87-20755
ISBN 0-8093-1421-5
ISBN 0-8093-1422-3 (pbk.)

Frank Lloyd Wright was a visionary who had his feet firmly planted on the ground. The architecture he created embraced the innovations of the future while respecting the needs and time-honored values of the American family. Since we have had the privilege of living in a home designed by Frank Lloyd Wright, my family and I have experienced firsthand the beauty and harmony of Wright's architecture.

This exhibition traces Wright's inspiration as it moves from the realm of ideas to an actual structure. By following the path of his creative process we can better understand how the design of the home influences the quality of life within it.

Whirlpool has long been a part of the American home and shares Frank Lloyd Wright's commitment to productive innovation. We are honored to co-sponsor this exhibition of America's preeminent architect, whose vision shapes residential architecture today and will continue to do so for generations to come.

Jack D. Sparks
*Chairman of the Board, President, and Chief Executive Officer*
*Whirlpool Corporation*

Frank Lloyd Wright believed that it was the nature of the human being to love and desire beauty and to live in it.

Certainly his creations embodied this need, and provided generations of human beings with a graciousness of living unsurpassed in his day. Taliesin, his home in Spring Green, Wisconsin, reflected his own desire for beauty and provided him with an environment that nurtured his amazing creative genius.

Kohler Co.'s abiding obligation, indeed its mission, is to produce products that provide a higher standard of gracious living for all economic levels. It is, therefore, with great pleasure that we co-sponsor an exhibition demonstrating Frank Lloyd Wright's principles of organic architecture.

We feel the exhibition effectively demonstrates not only Wright's cohesive style of architecture and design, but also his never-ending effort to add beauty, graciousness, and comfort to this world. It is a privilege to be able to help bring his message—a message shared by Kohler Co.—to all those who have an opportunity to see this exhibition of his works.

Herbert V. Kohler, Jr.
*Chairman of the Board and Chief Executive Officer*
*Kohler Co.*

# CONTENTS

# ⌘. ACKNOWLEDGMENTS

The organization of this project, the production of the book, the development of the exhibition, and the building of the Usonian Automatic Model House that will be included in the exhibition represent a labor of great devotion by scores of individuals. Not everyone who contributed important services to the enterprise can be recognized here, but the most salient contributors must be acknowledged.

The sponsors of the project have been crucial to its realization. The mayor and city council of Scottsdale, Arizona, took an early liking to the project and voted to buy the Usonian Automatic Model House as a permanent addition to the city center, where it will constitute a small museum devoted to the memory of Frank Lloyd Wright. Whirlpool Corporation and Kohler Co. joined in patronage to help realize the project and to provide for the national tour. Both organizations found a satisfying match between their corporate missions and Wright's drive to improve the standards of beauty and comfort in which the American family would live.

A number of other local and national companies with interest in the cultural significance of the exhibition and its tour have provided in-kind services to the enterprise, including: Whalen/Allied Van Lines, Milwaukee, shipping services; Landis Aerial Photography, Phoenix, photographic enlargements; Land O' Sun Printers, Scottsdale, brochure printing; Subiacolor, Tempe, mural transparencies; Pischoff Company, San Francisco, exhibition signage and graphic design; Whirlpool Kitchens, Inc., Englewood, Colorado, St. Charles cabinetry for the Usonian Automatic Model House; KitchenAid, Inc., St. Joseph, Michigan, major home appliances. In addition, local funding for the Phoenix-Scottsdale presentation was provided by Valley National Bank.

Special thanks are due to the lenders of objects of art to this long-running exhibition. I am grateful for the lenders' willingness to share with a national audience rare and valuable examples of Wright's designs from many decades. I want to extend a special salute to Domino's Pizza Collection, Ann Arbor, Michigan, for its generous assistance to the exhibition. I want also to express my gratitude to the other lenders: The Frank Lloyd Wright Foundation, Spring Green, Wisconsin; S. C. Johnson & Son, Racine, Wisconsin; the Johnson Foundation, also of Racine; the Darwin D. Martin House, Buffalo, New York; the Milwaukee Art Museum; Walter Netsch, Chicago; the Max Protetch Gallery, New York; the David and Alfred Smart Gallery, University of Chicago; and anonymous lenders.

Early in the development of the project an advisory committee was developed from the greater Phoenix community; this Scottsdale Arts Center Association committee has served dependably for more than two years. The names of the members are set out at the close of these remarks, but it must be recorded that every single member has made worthy contributions to the realization of the endeavor. Important early services were rendered by O. P. Reed, southern California art dealer and Wright enthusiast, in counseling the advisory committee and helping to frame the original concept of the project.

I must thank those colleagues who have given support to this endeavor in the most tangible and serious fashion: by electing to make it a part of their lives for the years over which it has grown, and by contracting to show the exhibition and the house in prime space and time during the national tour. These courageous museum professionals deserve our serious salute: Ms. Karen Bradley of the LTV Center Pavilion and Mr. Harry Parker of the Dallas Museum of Art; Mr. Roger Kennedy of the National Museum of American History, Washington, D.C.; Mr. Robert Frankel, Center for the Fine Arts, Miami, Florida; Dr. Victor Danilov, Museum of Science and Industry, Chicago, Illinois; our advisory committee member, Mr. Ron Caya, Director, Scottsdale Center for the Arts; and Mr. Steven L. Brezzo, Director, San Diego Museum of Art.

The following architects, staff members, and affiliates of the Frank Lloyd Wright Foundation are responsible for specific elements of the exhibition: general supervision and coordination, Richard E. Carney; selection of exhibition material, Bruce Brooks Pfeiffer; research and curatorial assistance, Indira Berndtson and Penny Fowler; planning and design of the exhibition, Anthony Puttnam, Susan Lockhart, Pamela Penn, and Oscar Munoz; model restoration, David Dodge; construction documents for and supervision of the Usonian Automatic Model House, E. T. Casey; audio/visual introduction, Anthony Puttnam; photography of the Frank Lloyd Wright drawings, Greg Williams, Simeon Posen, and Michael G. Mertz.

Finally, it is essential that the determined and facilitating efforts of one man, over more than thirty-six months, be recognized here. Lee Cohen's service as Chairman of the advisory committee has been an inspiration throughout our collaboration.

Gerald Nordland
*Curator of the exhibition*

SCOTTSDALE CITY COUNCIL

Herbert R. Drinkwater, *Mayor*    Bill Soderquist
Janes D. Bruner                   Bill Walton
Sam Kathryn Campana               Rene Wendell
Myron R. Deibel

SCOTTSDALE ARTS CENTER ASSOCIATION STEERING COMMITTEE FOR THE
FRANK LLOYD WRIGHT EXHIBITION, BOOK CATALOG, AND TOUR

Charles Allen, *Tempe*
James Ballinger, *Phoenix*
Indira Berndtson, *Taliesin*
Michael Boyles, *Tempe*
Richard E. Carney, *Taliesin*
E. Thomas Casey, *Taliesin*
Ron Caya, *Scottsdale*
George Christensen, *Phoenix*

Lee Cohen, *Scottsdale*
David Dodge, *Taliesin*
Ann Goldfein, *Tucson*
William A. Hicks III, *Paradise Valley*
David L. Lauer, *Kohler, Wisconsin*
Gerald Nordland, *Chicago*
Carl Park, *Phoenix*
Bruce Brooks Pfeiffer, *Taliesin*

Philippa Polskin, *New York City*
Anthony Puttnam, *Scottsdale*
Karen T. Scates, *Phoenix*
Adrienne Schiffner, *Phoenix*
Roger Schluntz, *Tempe*
Lenard F. Schweitzer, *Benton Harbor,
    Michigan*
K. Paul Zygas, *Scottsdale*

SCOTTSDALE ARTS CENTER ASSOCIATION BOARD OF DIRECTORS 1987—88
*Denotes Executive Committee*

David B. Arriola
Dorothy (Wink) Blair
William H. Carlile
Kenneth M. Carpenter
Donna B. Chrisco—*Vice-President, Development*
*Anne Christensen—*Vice-President, Programming*
*Lee Cohen
*Lydia F. D'Agosto—*Vice-President, Service*
Richard D. Dunseath
John Fahrendorf, Jr.
Penny Galarneau
*Pam Hait—*Secretary*
*William A. Hicks III
William Huizingh—*Treasurer*
*Kenneth Husband—*President*

Ruth Kaspar
*Richard B. Kelly
William D. Long
*Don Martin
Mary Mayfield
Martin O'Sullivan
D. Michael Rappoport
Lester Rossin
Martin Schenk
Favour Slater
Joe Sparks
*Carlos E. Wagner
Carolyn S. Allen—*Executive Director*
Suzette Arnold Lucas—*Administrator*

# PREFACE

On June 8, 1967, several organizations across the United States celebrated a Frank Lloyd Wright "centennial." Since Mr. Wright always considered 1869 the year of his birth, we his heirs at the Taliesin Fellowship—including Mr. Wright's widow, Olgivanna Lloyd Wright—celebrated another "centennial" on June 8, 1969. At that occasion, held at Taliesin West, there were several speeches by some of the many friends and guests there assembled. One was by Mrs. Wright, who told us that the truly important event would not be Mr. Wright's centennial but his bicentennial. "One hundred years from now," she said, "people will look at his ideas, his principles, his forms, and see—with wonder and amazement—that those ideas are still fresh, vibrant, applicable, and intensely prophetic. That will be the remarkable occasion—two hundred years after his birth—to see those ideas and that work still alive and looking into the future."

Architecturally, we are living in the age of Frank Lloyd Wright, the father of modern architecture. That age has been with us since Mr. Wright started his practice in 1893. Time seems to expand and contract in unpredictable ways until we realize that time has no real bearing on any matter of real import. It is nothing more than a measuring device, like an architect's scale. The impact that Frank Lloyd Wright has had on architecture in this century will surely go on into further centuries, not only because the forms themselves are so timeless, but above all because his ideas remain so vibrant.

Using Frank Lloyd Wright's work as example and his own words as explanatory text, this book and this exhibition endeavor to highlight and illustrate those ideas that constitute the foundation upon which everything he designed and built is based. The sole purpose for compiling both the book and the exhibition is to generate an understanding of ideas, not forms. The forms shown here are unmistakably and irrevocably Mr. Wright's. But the ideas will be a never-ending source of inspiration for the future of architecture as subsequent generations of architects create their own forms.

Bruce Brooks Pfeiffer
*January 30, 1987*

# FRANK LLOYD WRIGHT
# IN THE REALM OF IDEAS

# INTRODUCTION

*Gerald Nordland*

. . . architecture which was really architecture proceeded from the ground and . . . somehow the terrain, the native industrial conditions, the nature of materials, and the purpose of the building.

FRANK LLOYD WRIGHT, *First London Lecture,* 1939

The initial idea for this publication and the 1988–90 exhibition of the same title arose out of meetings between the president of the Scottsdale Arts Center Association (SACA) and representatives of the Frank Lloyd Wright Foundation in 1984. Lee Cohen, then president of the support group of the Scottsdale Center for the Arts and a former student of architecture, believed that a major exhibition of Frank Lloyd Wright material would be a unique service to Scottsdale and the nation. Richard Carney, Managing Trustee of the Foundation, and Bruce Brooks Pfeiffer, Director of Archives, agreed, and a dialogue began. An advisory committee was created around

Gerald Nordland is an art critic and museum director. He studied at the University of Southern California, receiving B.A. and J.D. degrees. He has contributed to many national and international art magazines, and has served as Art Critic for *Frontier* magazine and the *Los Angeles* (Times) *Mirror.* He has been director of the Washington Gallery of Modern Art, the San Francisco Museum of Modern Art, the Frederick S. Wight Art Galleries at UCLA, and the Milwaukee Art Museum. He has recently received a Guggenheim Fellowship and is preparing a book on Richard Diebenkorn for Rizzoli International.

SACA and the Frank Lloyd Wright Foundation, including community leaders interested and experienced in cultural and artistic events, the then president of the A.I.A., practicing architects, a group of faculty (including the dean) of the Arizona State University School of Architecture, and representatives of the Phoenix Art Museum.

An early decision of the committee was to focus on the principles underlying Frank Lloyd Wright's architecture rather than solely on his buildings, and to confine the interpretive words in the exhibition (now Part I of this book) to the speeches and writings of Wright himself. With the exception of such decorative items as chairs and windows—a selection of such items appears in Appendix B—Part I reproduces all the works displayed in the exhibition. Like the exhibition itself, Part I is organized according to what the committee deemed to be Wright's four most important contributions to the theory and practice of architecture in the twentieth century.

The subject of the first section is probably his single most important idea: what he called "the destruction of the box." He found the fundamentals of the idea in his Larkin Building (Buffalo, 1904) when he pushed the staircase towers out from the corners of the main space and made them free-standing features. He carried the idea further with his Unity Temple (Oak Park, Illinois, 1904), in which he used clerestory windows and walls as mere screens dividing space that was free. Soon he was building houses in which the span between the corners was reduced by moving the vertical supports inward and leaving the corners open, thus making the walls screens again and letting the outside reciprocally flow inward. Since what he had done horizontally could also be done vertically, the classical box was no longer necessary. When walls became independent screens, "the open plan appeared naturally; the relationship of inhabitants to the outside became more intimate; landscape and building became one, more harmonious; and instead of a separate thing set up independently of landscape and site, the building with landscape and site became inevitably one."

The second section of Part I deals with Wright's unusual sensitivity to the available plot of ground for a given structure. The architect designed and built entirely differently for the urban street than for the country acre, the open glen, the desert, and the oceanside. He had quick responses to the problems and advantages of a site and let those responses govern his designs and his choice of materials. The site and the needs of the client were brought together into a single solution. The materials chosen for the building were inevitably related to the structure's purpose and the techniques best calculated to provide satisfactory performance within financial limits. Where vistas were beautiful, Wright took advantage of their beauty, inviting it inward and extending the inhabitant's vision outward wherever possible. Where they were not beautiful, he turned the focus inward, away from the industrial landscape or the ravaged factory neighborhood, to make a handsome, comfortable, healthful interior environment conducive to productive work.

Wright often advised clients not to build on the top of a hill, but instead, after first deciding what view of the hill they liked best, to build around the brow of the hill in such a way as to preserve that view after the building was erected. He also was known to tell clients to choose sites far out from the city, beyond the distance they felt acceptable, saying the sites would soon enough be close to town. He even advised clients to purchase problem lots, sites with character but with features many architects would consider crippling drawbacks. Such sites challenged Wright to find unorthodox ways of meeting the needs of the client, and provoked some of his best creative work.

Wright was one of the first designers and architects to proclaim the value of the machine and the simplified and direct use of materials, and this is the subject of Part I's third section. In his lecture at Hull House on "The Art and Craft of the Machine" and later in his Princeton lectures of 1930, he proclaimed architecture as "the triumph of human imagination over materials, methods and men, to put man into possession of his earth." "Bring out the nature of materials, let their nature intimately into your schemes . . . reveal the nature of the wood, plaster, brick or stone in your designs; they are all by nature friendly and beautiful." Each building material, he thought, had certain properties and beauties that made it particularly appropriate for certain projects. Each had its own grammar, which was different from every other, and each had to be handled in its own special way. He maintained that earlier generations had used materials interchangeably without sensitivity to their individual natures.

In Wright's view, our civilization's true record would be written in scientific theorems made operative in iron and steel and in the manufacturing processes that characterize the new machine age. "The machine is a marvelous simplifier . . . and may be the modern emancipator of the creative mind." Using the machine to mimic handwork is wrong. "The machines used in woodwork [for example] will show that by unlimited power in cutting, shaping, smoothing and by the tireless repeat they have emancipated beauties of wood nature, making possible without waste, beautiful surface treatments and clean strong forms that veneers of Sheraton or Chippendale only hinted at with dire extravagance." "These machines have undoubtedly placed within reach of the designer a technique enabling him to realize the true nature of wood in his designs harmoniously with man's sense of beauty, satisfying his materials need with such extraordinary economy as to put the beauty of wood in use within the reach of everyone." The same creative analysis had to be made for each material—plaster, stone, glass, steel, each had its own special characteristics and distinctive grammar.

Writing of designing for the machine, both in architecture and in the design of interior fittings, Wright continued: "I wanted to realize genuine new forms true to the spirit of great tradition and found I should have to make them; not only make forms appropriate to the old (natural) and to the new (synthetic) materials, but I should have to so design them that the machine (or process) that must make them could and would make them better than anything could possibly be made by hand."

Within a structure, "the ideal of 'organic simplicity' seen as the countenance of perfect integration . . . naturally abolished all fixtures, rejected the old furnishings . . . declared them to be irrelevant or superficial decoration. The new practice made all furnishings so far as possible, (certainly the electric light-ing and heating systems), integral parts of the architecture. So far as possible all furniture was to be designed in place as part of the building. Hangings, rugs, carpets, were they to be used (as they might be if properly designed) all came into the same category. . . .

"Inevitably this deeper sense of building as integral produce of the spirit of man is to construct the physical body of our machine age. But that in itself will not be enough. Unless this construction were to enable a broader, finer sense of life as something to be lived into the full, all resources of time, place and man in place to give us an architecture that is inspiring environment at the same time it is a true expression of that life itself, the ideal will again have failed."

The fourth section of Part I explores one of Wright's most frequently expressed aspirations: to produce an architecture properly suited to a free society. He was confident that every society produces—in the long run—an architecture reflective of its life, its time, and its values. He felt this was logically similar to permitting the function of the building to be manifested in its architectural form rather than subjected to the dreary sameness of international-style building forms. *Form and function had to become one*. Ultimately Wright came to feel that his oeuvre was moving toward an encyclopedic inclusiveness that would reflect the democratic nature of modern American life. He saw his Broadacre City visions and all his built and unbuilt projects as part of a single fabric, a new American architectural idiom from which he could point the way toward a genuinely democratic, free, and independent life.

Wright envisioned the simple private home as one whose owners were secure on their own property; had as large a living room as they could afford, open to garden and light and equipped with a fireplace and bookshelves; had a dining area with built-ins and an adjacent odorless kitchen; and had, among other things, room to grow in. All the furnishings and plantings were to be designed by the architect and subject to the architect's oversight to ensure quality and harmony. Free and open spaces, multiple uses, the indoor-outdoor life to be enjoyed on one's own plot of land: it was a political and economic declaration of independence for the common citizen.

In the same spirit, Wright saw the industrial or office workspace as a humane and prideful environment, convenient of access, healthful, air-conditioned, and well-lighted. Civic buildings, courthouses, churches, and entertainment centers were conceived in the same spirit, encouraging freedom, fostering choice, celebrating mobility. The Broadacre City concept was an early exemplification of the unity he envisioned for city and country, farm and factory, private dwellings and schools, parks and government services—each and all designed with regard for the individual and the group.

Part II of the present volume consists of essays on the state of architecture in the United States at the time Wright began to practice; his conceptual contributions to modern architecture, notably "organic architecture" and "engineering architecture"; the educational and philosophical backgrounds of Wright's view of democracy; and the part his wife Olgivanna took in the founding of the Taliesin Fellowship and in its administration during Wright's life and after his death.

The precision and grace of Frank Lloyd Wright's architecture are rarely to be found in his writing. He wrote swiftly and with ardor, and although he revised some pieces from time to time, his ideas were so large and encompassing that he found it sufficient if his words conveyed their general shape or effect. Surely no one of his time thought more deeply about the functions and possibilities of architecture, and there is no better record of that thinking than his own words. Though his monument is unquestionably what he designed and built, there is much still to be learned from what he wrote.

PART ONE

IDEAS AND IMAGES

All words quoted in Part I are the words of Frank Lloyd Wright. Sources for individual passages, keyed by page number, are given in Appendix A. Full information about the works pictured, also keyed by page number, is given in Appendix B.

# ▣. WHAT IS ARCHITECTURE?

What is architecture anyway? Is it the vast collection of the various buildings which have been built to please the varying taste of the various lords of mankind? I think not. No, I know that architecture is life; or at least it is life itself taking form and therefore it is the truest record of life as it was lived in the world yesterday, as it is lived today or ever will be lived. So architecture I know to be a Great Spirit. . . . Architecture is that great living creative spirit which from generation to generation, from age to age, proceeds, persists, creates, according to the nature of man, and his circumstances as they change. That is really architecture.

I still believe that the ideal of an organic architecture forms the origin and source, the strength and, fundamentally, the significance of everything ever worthy the name of architecture.

By organic architecture I mean an architecture that *develops* from within outward in harmony with the conditions of its being as distinguished from one that is *applied* from without.

As we pass along the wayside some blossom with unusually glowing color or prettiness of form attracts us. Held by it we gratefully accept its perfect loveliness. But, seeking the secret of its ineffable charm, we find that the blossom, whose more obvious claim first arrested our attention, as nature intended, is intimately related to the texture and shape of the foliage beneath. We discover peculiar sympathy between the form of this flower and the system upon which leaves are arranged about the stalk. From this we are led on to observe a characteristic habit of growth and discover a resultant pattern of structure. . . . *Structure* —as now we may observe—proceeds from generals to particulars arriving at the blossom, to attract us, proclaiming in its lines and form the nature of the structure that bore it. We have here a thing *organic*. Law and order are the basis of a finished grace and beauty. Beauty is the expression of fundamental conditions in line, form and color true to those conditions and seeming to exist to fulfill them according to some thoughtful original design.

Organic simplicity might everywhere be seen producing significant character in the ruthless but harmonious order I was taught to call nature. I was more than familiar with it on the farm. All around me, I, or anyone for that matter, might see beauty in growing things and, by a little painstaking, learn how they grew to be beautiful. None was ever insignificant.

Only by patient study, to acquire knowledge of nature *in this interior sense*, are guiding principles ever to be established by the architect. Ideals gained by comprehension of these *or-*

*ganic* limitations are never lost. An artist having these may then defy his education. If he is really for nature in this inward sense he may be a rebel against his time and its laws but never lawless in his work nor as himself.

The architect must be the most comprehensive of all the masters, most comprehensive of all the human beings on earth. His work, the thing that is entrusted to him by way of his virtue, is the most broad of all.

# THE DESTRUCTION OF THE BOX:
# THE FREEDOM OF SPACE

Down all the avenues of time architecture was an enclosure by nature, and the simplest form of enclosure was the box. The box was ornamented, they put columns in front of it, pilasters and cornices on it, but they always considered an enclosure in terms of the box. Now when Democracy became an establishment, as it is in America, that box-idea began to be irksome. As a young architect, I began to feel annoyed, held back, imposed upon by this sense of enclosure which you went into and there you were—boxed, crated. I tried to find out what was happening to me: I was the free son of a free people and I wanted to be free. I had to find out what was the cause of this imprisonment. So I began to investigate.

I think I first *consciously* began to try to beat the box in the Larkin Building—1906. I found a natural opening to the liberation I sought when (after a great struggle) I finally pushed the staircase towers out from the corners of the main building, made them into free-standing, individual features . . . (to let the light and air in at the corners). . . . I had *felt* this need for features quite early in my architectural life. You will see this feeling growing up, becoming more apparent a little later in Unity Temple: there perhaps is where you will find the first real expression of the idea that the space within the building is the reality of that building. . . . So that sense of freedom began which has come into the architecture of today for you and which we call organic architecture.

The conception of the room *within*, the interior spaces of the building to be conserved, expressed and made living as architecture—the architecture of the *within*—that is precisely what we are driving at, all along. And this new quality of thought in architecture, the third dimension, let us say, enters into every move that is made to make it—enters into the use of every material; enters the working of every method we shall use or can use.

The box did not fulfill the possibilities of steel and glass. Steel—the new material—allowed tenuity. Now you could make the building tough with tensile strength. If the idea was to do away with the box, here was the means. There now came the cantilever. You could put the load under the center of the beam or you could reduce the span between the corners by moving the supports inward and leaving the corner open. In that single circumstance—what I suppose would be called engineering—came the opportunity to destroy the box. . . . Walls could be screens independent of each other; the open plan appeared naturally; the relationship of inhabitants to the outside became more intimate; landscape and building become one, more harmonious. . . . So the life of the individual was broadened and enriched by the new concept of architecture, by light and freedom of space.

*Guggenheim Museum*

←

The eye encounters no abrupt change, but is gently led and treated as if at the edge of the shore watching an unbreaking wave. . . . Here for the first time architecture appears plastic, one floor flowing into another instead of the usual superimposition of stratified layers cutting and butting into each other by post and beam construction.

→

Here we are not building a cellular composition of compartments, but one where all is one great space on a single continuous floor. . . . Let walls, ceilings, floors become seen as component parts of each other.

*Guggenheim Museum*

*Guggenheim Museum Model*

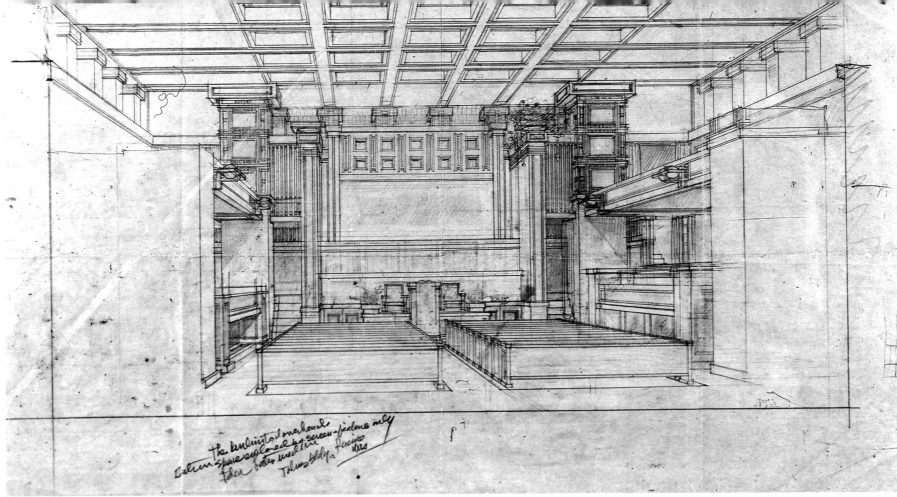

The unlimited overhead. Interior space enclosed by screen-features only. Idea later used in Johnson Bldg, Racino.

*Unity Temple*

↑  The unlimited overhead. Interior space enclosed by screen-features only. Idea later used in Johnson Bldg, Racine.

←  It is not to subjugate the paintings to the building that I conceived this plan. On the contrary, it was to make the building and the painting an uninterrupted, beautiful symphony such as never existed in the World of Art before.

→  With Unity Temple there were no walls of any kind, only features. And the features were screens grouped about interior space. . . . When I finished Unity Temple, I had it. I knew I had the beginning of a great thing, a great truth in architecture. Now architecture could be free.

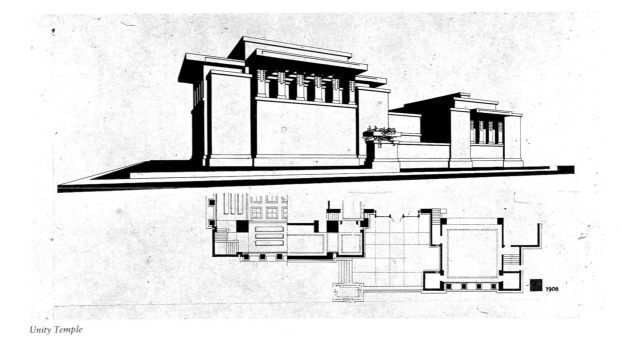

*Unity Temple*

*Johnson Administration Building*

←

There in the Johnson Building you catch no sense of enclosure whatever at any angle, top or sides. . . . Interior space comes free, you are not aware of any boxing in at all. Restricted space simply is not there. Right there where you've always experienced this interior constriction you take a look at the sky!

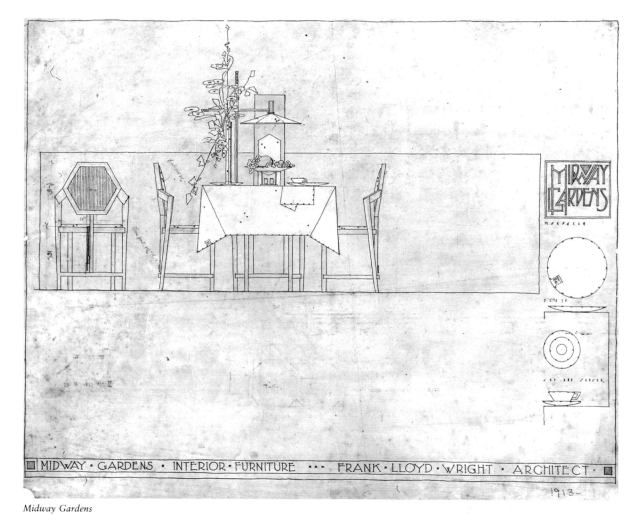

*Midway Gardens*

→

Site, structure, furnishing—decoration too, planting as well—all these become as one in organic architecture.

There were no plans like these in existence at
the time but my clients were pushed towards
these ideas as helpful to a solution of the vexed
servant problem. Scores of unnecessary doors dis-
appeared and no end of partition. Both clients
and servants liked the new freedom. The house
became more free as space and more livable, too.
Interior spaciousness began to dawn.

*Coonley House*

*Coonley House*

*Coonley House*

*"Taliesin West"*

← The song, the masterpiece, the edifice are a warm outpouring of the heart of man—human delight in life triumphant: we glimpse the infinite. That glimpse or vision is what makes art a matter of inner experience—therefore sacred, and no less but rather more individual in this age, I assure you, than ever before.

→ Making away with the box both in plan and elevation now became fundamental to my work. That opened the way for feeling the space within as the Reality of all true modern building. . . . These structures now bear the message of this liberation of space to space.

*"Taliesin West"*

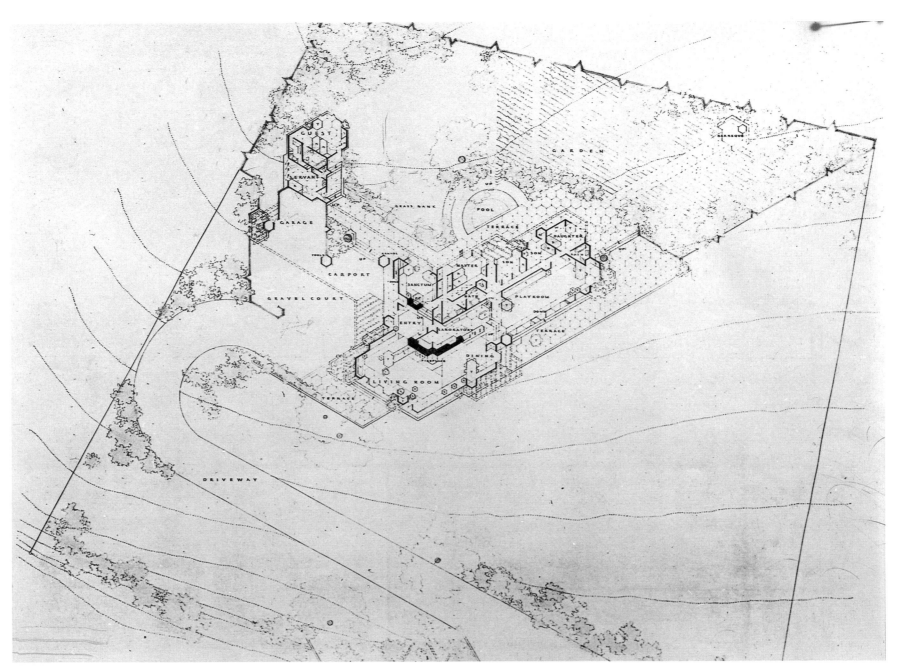

*Hanna House*

Modern architecture rejects the major axis and the minor axis of classic architecture. It rejects all grandomania, every building that would stand in military fashion heels together, eyes front, something on the right hand and something on the left hand. Architecture already favors the reflex, the natural easy attitude, the occult symmetry of grace and rhythm affirming the ease, grace, and naturalness of natural life.

*Hanna House*

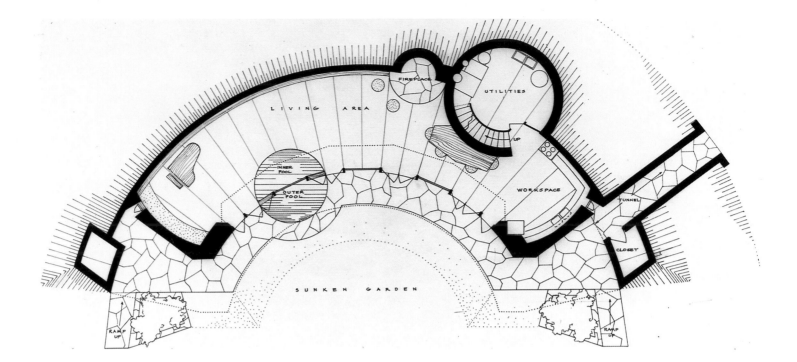

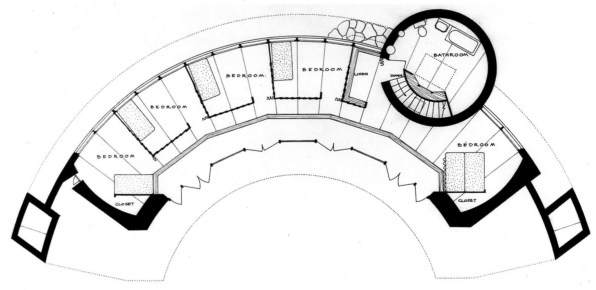

As interior space to be lived in becomes the reality of building, so shelter thus emphasized becomes more than ever significant in character and important as a feature. . . . The new sense of spaciousness requires, as inherent human factor, significant cover as well as shade. . . . Weather is omnipresent and buildings must be left out in the rain. Shelter is dedicated to these elements. So much so that almost all other features of design tend to lead by one another to this important feature, shelter, and its component shade. . . . By shade, charm has been added to character; style to comfort; significance to form.

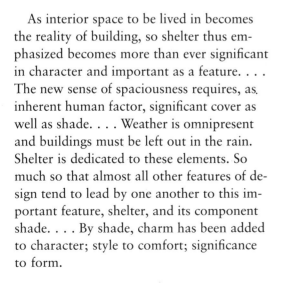

*Jacobs House*

Jacobs House

*"Sijistan" Project*

← 

Furnishings should be consistent in design and construction, and used with style as an extension in the sense of the building which they "furnish." Wherever possible all should be natural. The sure reward for maintaining these simple features of architectural integrity is great serenity.

→

Organic architecture sees the third dimension never as weight or mere thickness but always as *depth*. Depth an element of space; the third (or thickness) dimension transformed into a *space* dimension.

. . . A true liberation of life and light within walls; a new structural integrity; outside coming in; and the space within, to be lived in, going out. Space outside becomes a natural part of space *within* the building. . . . Walls are now apparent more as humanized screens. They do define and differentiate, but never confine or obliterate. A new sense of reality in building construction has arrived.

*"Fallingwater" (Edgar J. Kaufmann House)*

*"Fallingwater"*

*"Crownfield" (Robert F. Windfohr House)*

Profoundly natural, these buildings are never dull or monotonous because this subtle quality of integrity due to "the each in each and the each in all" is continually there although not tangible to any superficial view.

→

The essence of organic building is space, space flowing outward, space flowing inward. Both plan and construction are seen to be inspired from within.

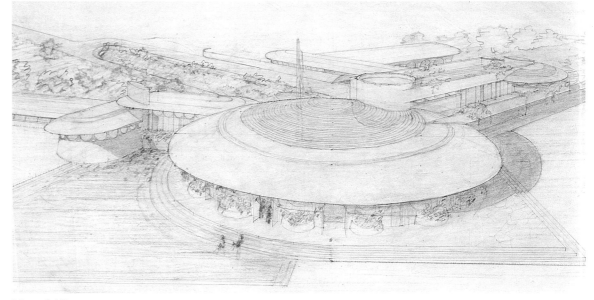

*"Crownfield"*

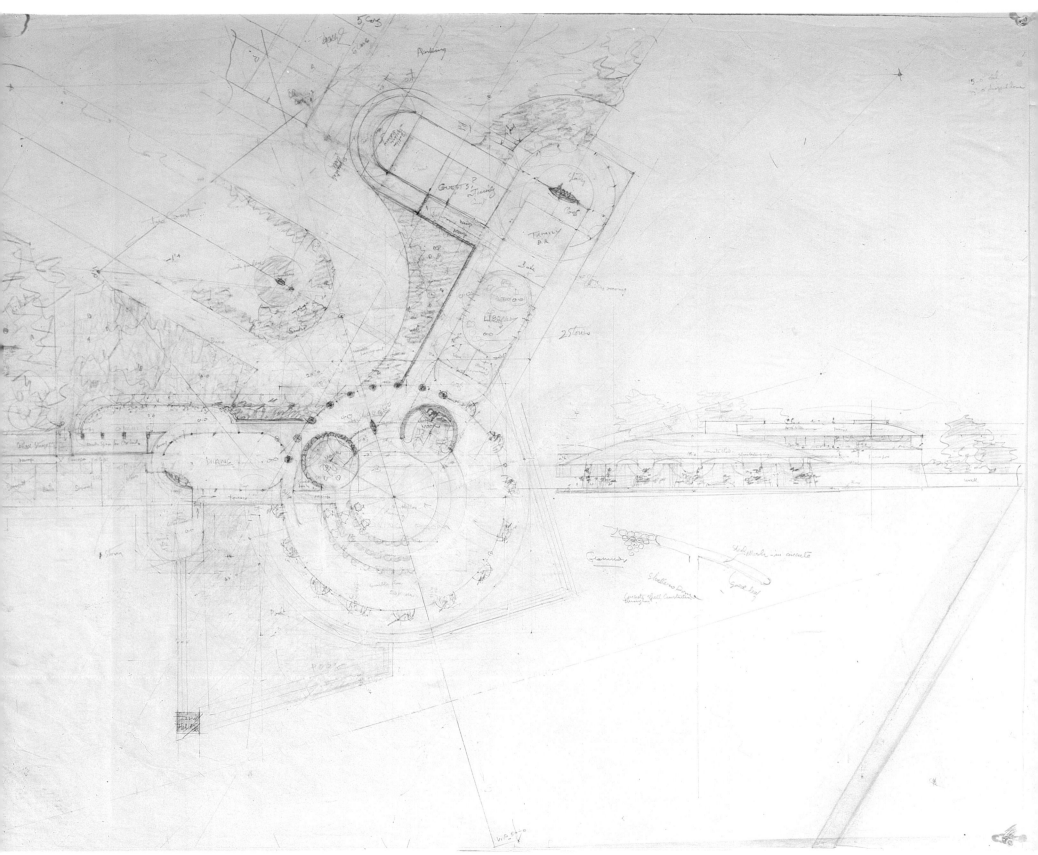

*"Crownfield"*

# ◲. THE NATURE OF THE SITE

Man takes a positive hand in creation whenever he puts a building upon the earth beneath the sun. If he has birthright at all, it must consist in this: that he, too, is no less a feature of the landscape than the rocks, trees, bears or bees of that nature to which he owes his being.

Building is an organism only if in accord outside with inside and both with the character and nature of its purpose, process, place and time. It will then incorporate the nature of the site, of the methods by which it is constructed, and finally the whole—from grade to coping, ground to skyline—will be becoming to its purpose.

This is all merely the common-sense of organic architecture.

→ Arizona character seems to cry out for a space-loving architecture of its own. The straight line and flat plane must come here—of all places—but they should become the dotted line, the broad, low, extended plane textured, because in all this astounding desert there is not one hard undotted line to be seen.

And what of the subsidence we see now in the streamlines of these endless ranges of mountains coming gently down to the mesa or going abruptly up into the sky from the plains. In this geologic era, catastrophic upheaval has found comparative repose; to these vast, quiet, ponderable masses made so by fire and laid by water—both are architects—now comes the sculptor, wind. Wind and water ceaselessly eroding, endlessly working to quiet and harmonize all traces of violence until a glorious unison is again bathed in the atmosphere of a light that is, it must be, eternal.

*"Taliesin West"*

*home just completed for the Pauson Sisters Phoenix Arizona*

*Pauson House*

A desert building should be nobly simple in outline as the region itself is sculptured.

*Pew House*

A house, we like to believe, can be a noble consort to man and the trees; therefore the house should have repose and such texture as will quiet the whole and make it graciously at one with external nature.

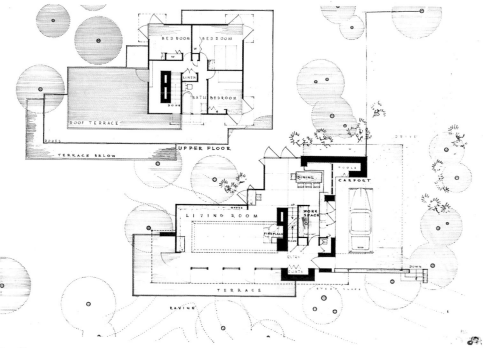

*Pew House*

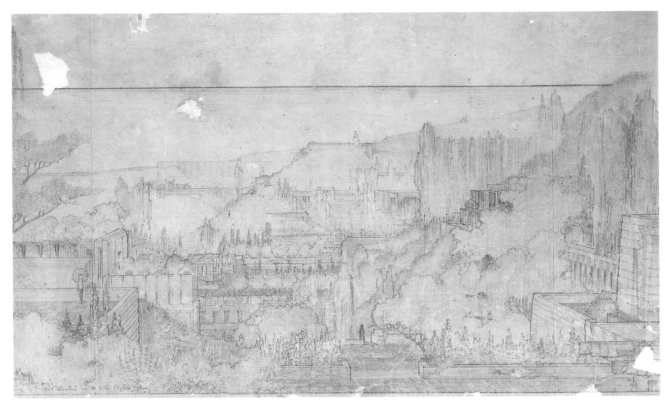

*Doheny Ranch Resort Project*

When organic architecture is properly carried out no landscape is ever outraged by it but is always developed by it.

*Doheny Ranch Resort Project*

*Doheny Ranch Resort Project*

*Affleck House Model*

A good site . . . at the most difficult spot . . . one that has features . . . individuality.

*V. C. Morris Shop*

*V. C. Morris Shop*

The character of the site is always fundamental to organic design.

*Robie House*

In breadth, length, height and weight, these buildings belonged to the prairie just as the human being himself belonged to it with his gift of speed. The term "streamlined" as my own expression was then and there born. As result, the new buildings were rational: low, swift, and clean, and were studiously adapted to machine methods.

The human figure appeared to me, about 1893 or earlier, as the true *human* scale of architecture. Buildings I myself then designed and built—Midwest—seemed, by means of this new scale, to belong to man and at the moment especially as he lived on the rolling Western prairie.

The main objective was gracious appropriation of the art of architecture itself to the Time, the Place, and Modern Man. What now is organic "design"? Design appropriate to modern tools, the machine, and this new human scale.

*Robie House*

*Masieri Memorial Project*

Loving Venice as I do I wanted, by way of modern techniques, to make old Venice tradition live anew. . . . What I have done, as you will see, is no ruthless sacrifice of an ancient culture to a modern ambition, but is, I am sure, a worthy tribute to you all and harmonious with your great Tradition . . .

*Masieri Memorial Project*

*Marin County Civic Center*

An axiom: the solution of every problem is contained within itself. Its
plan, form and character are determined by the nature of the site.

BARNSDALL HOUSE 1913

*"Hollyhock House" (Aline Barnsdall House)*

↑

Hollyhock House was to be a natural house . . . naturally built; native to the region of California. Suited to Miss Barnsdall and her purpose, such a house would be sure to be all that "poetry of form" could imply, because any house should be beautiful in California in the way that California herself is beautiful.

→

Up there on Olive Hill above hillsides furrowed with rows of gray-green olive trees, the daughter of one of America's pioneers had constructed a little principality of her very own, free to live in it as a queen.

In any expression of the human spirit it is principle manifest as character that alone endures. Individuality is the true property of character.

*"Hollyhock House"*

*"Hollyhock House"*

Grammar of building related to character of prospect and region.

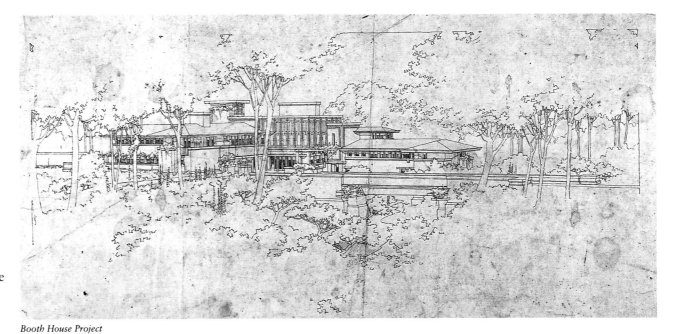

*Booth House Project*

The good building makes the landscape more beautiful than it was before that building was built.

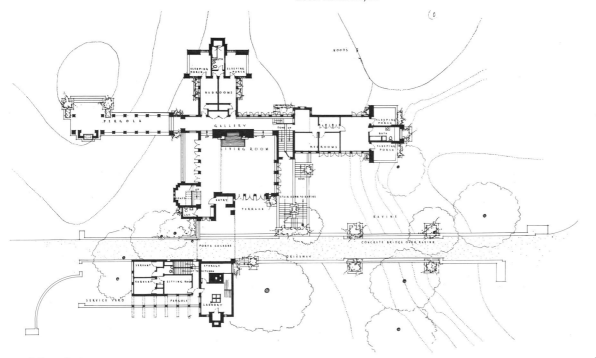

*Booth House Project*

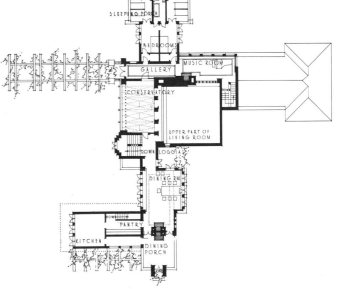

*Booth House Project*

*Booth House Project*

*"Fallingwater"* (Edgar J. Kaufmann House)

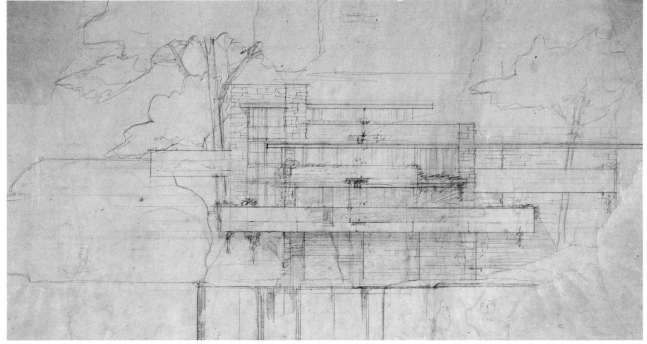

"Fallingwater"

We got down into that glen to associate with and play with the natural stream . . .

"No, not simply to look at the waterfalls but to live with them . . ."

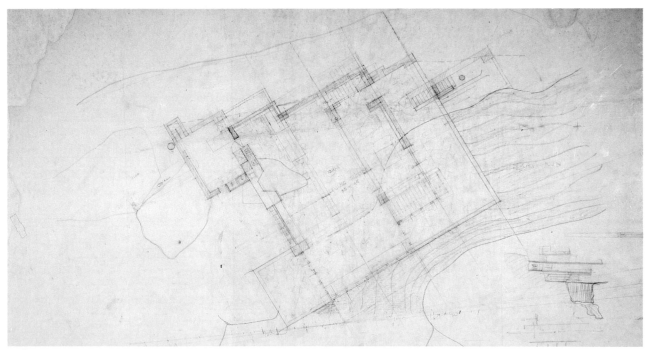

"Fallingwater"

Fallingwater is a great blessing—one of the great blessings to be experienced here on earth. I think nothing yet ever equalled the coordination, sympathetic expression of the great principle of repose where forest and stream and rock and all the elements of structure are combined so quietly that really you listen not to any noise whatsoever although the music of the stream is there. But you listen to Fallingwater the way you listen to the quiet of the country . . .

*Walker House*

My prescription for a modern house: first, a good site. Pick one that has features making for character. . . . Then build your house so that you may still look from where you stood upon all that charmed you and lose nothing of what you saw before the house was built, but see more.

→ →

Architectural association accentuates the character of the landscape if the architecture is right.

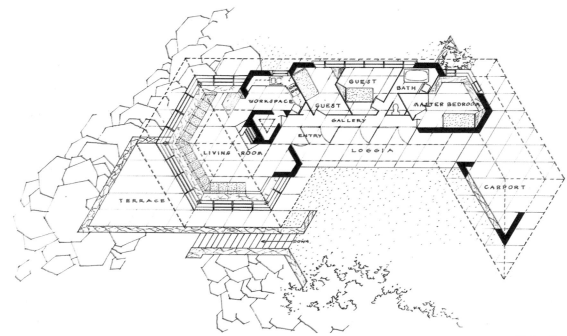

*Walker House*

VIEW FROM NORTHEAST
POINT VIEW RESIDENCES
FOR THE EDGAR J. KAUFMANN CHARITABLE TRUST
FRANK LLOYD WRIGHT ARCHITECT

*Bailleres House Project*

These ideals when put into practice take the buildings out of school and marry them to the ground; make them all intimate expressions (or revelations) of interiors and individualize them regardless of preconceived notions of Style. I have tried to make their grammar perfect in its way and to give their forms and proportions integrity that will bear study although few of them can be intelligently studied apart from environment.

*Gerts House Project*

I loved the prairie by instinct as, itself, a great simplicity; the trees, flowers and sky were thrilling by contrast. And I saw that a little of height on the prairie was enough to look like much more. Notice how every detail as to height becomes intensely significant and how breadths all fall short.

In considering the various forms and types of these structures, the fact that nearly all were buildings for our vast Western prairie should be borne in mind; the gently rolling or level prairies of our great Middle West; the great rolling prairies where every detail of elevation becomes exaggerated; every tree towers above the great calm plains of flowered surfaces as the plain lies serene beneath a wonderful unlimited sweep of sky. . . . More intimate relation with outdoor environment and far-reaching vista is sought to balance the desired lessening of height.

# ▣. MATERIALS AND METHODS

Architecture is the triumph of human imagination over materials, methods and men, to put man into possession of his own earth.

Machinery, materials and men—yes—these are the stuffs by means of which the so-called American architect will get his architecture. . . . Only by the strength of his spirit's grasp upon all three—machinery, materials and men—will the architect be able so to build that his work may be worthy the great name architecture.

Bring out the nature of the materials, let their nature intimately into your scheme. . . . Reveal the nature of the wood, plaster, brick or stone in your designs; they are all by nature friendly and beautiful.

The machine can be nowhere creator except as it may be a good tool in the creative artist's tool box. It is only when you try to make a living thing of the machine itself that you begin to betray your human birthright. The machine can do great work—yes—but only when well in the hand of one who does not overestimate its resources, one who knows how to put it to suitable work for the human being.

Now there can be nothing frozen or static about either the methods or effects of organic architecture. All must be the spontaneous reaction of the creative mind to a specific problem in the nature of materials.

→

*Stone,* as a building material, as human hands begin upon it—stonecraft—becomes a shapely block. The block is necessarily true to square and level, so that one block may securely rest upon another block and great weight be carried to greater height.

We refer to such masses, so made, as masonry.

*"Taliesin"*

*Imperial Hotel*

Stone is inforescent: stone is the mass residue of intense heat. Stone is therefore the simplest mass material. As human hands directed by imagination being upon it, it becomes a shapely block. The wall will be determined by the character of the stone if the work is to be good stonework.

The stone may show a natural face in the wall, or a face characteristic of the tool used to shape it.

The character of the wall-surface will be determined also by the kind of stone, by the kind of mason, the kind of architect.

Brick is the ground you tread upon turned by fire
into something to use to build.

*Larkin Administration Building*

*Larkin Administration Building*

The Larkin Building is the first great protestant against the out-
rageous elaboration of the period. An affirmative negation, however.
It is the simple, dignified direct utterance of a plain, utilitarian type,
with sheer brick walls and the indispensable protective stone-copings
this climate demands.

*Sturges House*

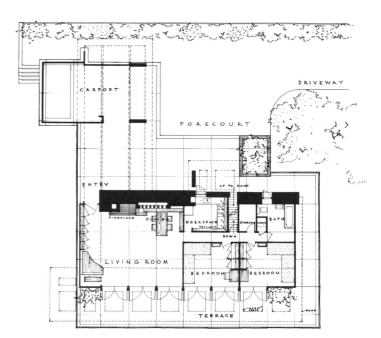

*Sturges House*

Make the walls of brick that fire touched to tawny gold or ruddy tan,
choicest of all earth's hues.

*Heurtley House*

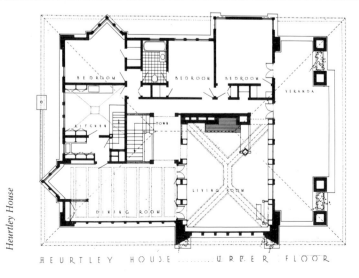

HEURTLEY HOUSE ....... UPPER FLOOR

We probably have brought brick-making to a pitch of perfection never existing in the world before. . . . Not only is the range inexhaustible in texture and color and shape, but the material itself is admirable in quality.

*Jester House Project Model*

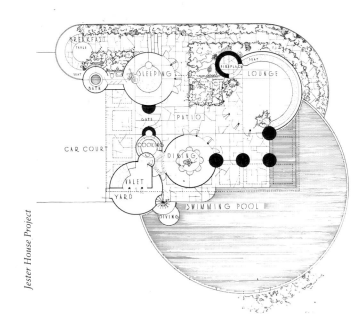

The tree is a flower of light. Wood is true efflorescence; extroversion subject to light, and organic growth responding to heat. Wood is the most humanly intimate and of all materials the most kindly to man.

*Pew House*

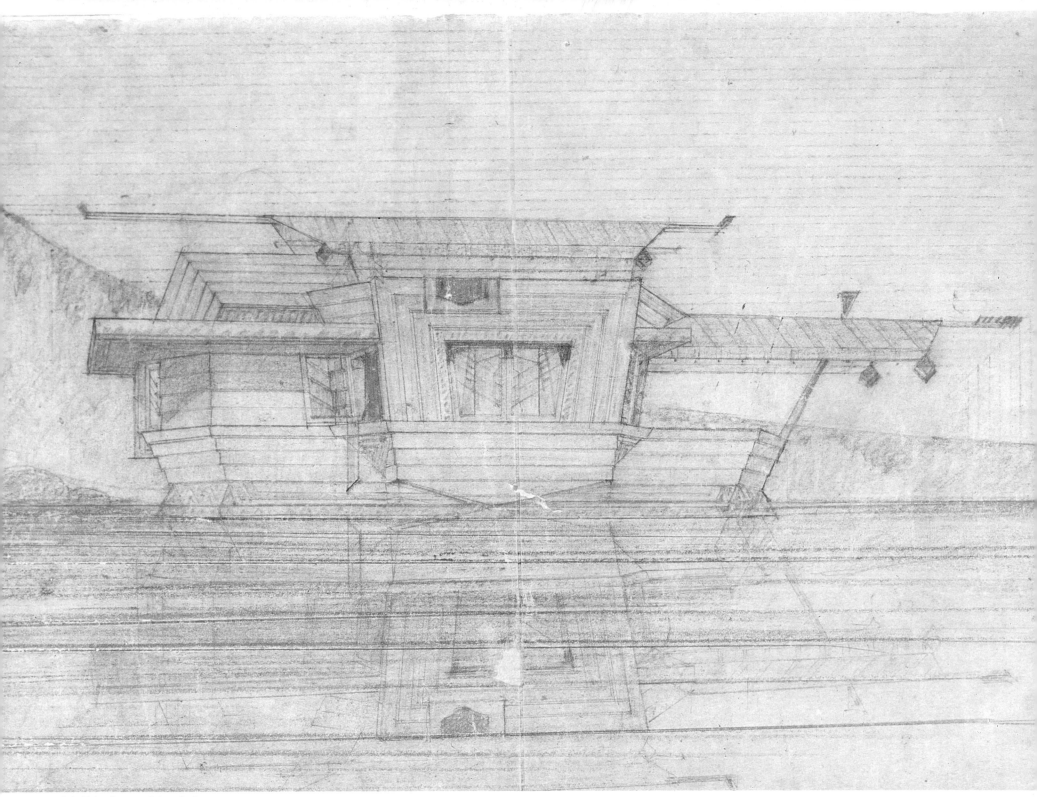

*Lake Tahoe Summer Colony Project*

*Stamm Boathouse Project*

Wood is universally beautiful to man. . . . Man loves his association with it; likes to feel it under his hand, sympathetic to his touch and to his eye.

*Stamm Boathouse Project*

*"Cedar Rock" (Lowell Walter House)*

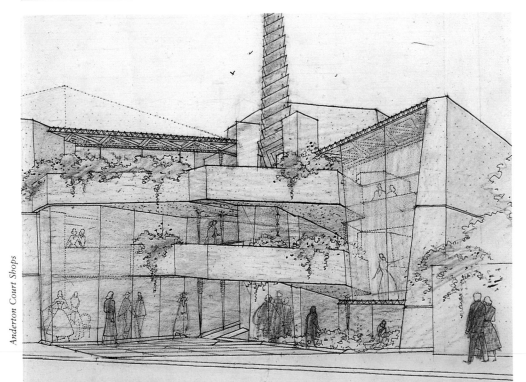

Glass surfaces, too, may be modified to let the vision sweep through to any extent up to perfection.

Glass has now a perfect visibility, thin sheets of air crystallized to keep air currents outside or inside.

*Johnson Administration Building*

Let the modern now work with light, light diffused, light reflected, light refracted—light for its own sake, shadows gratuitous.

→

More and more, light began to become the beautifier of the building—the blessing of the occupants.

*Beth Sholom Synagogue*

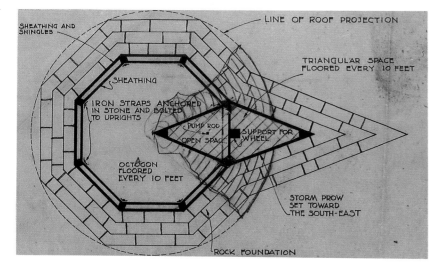

*"Romeo and Juliet" Windmill Tower*

My first engineering-architecture, 1896. New type of engineering construction; the streamlined form of a structure is based on the penetration of a hexagon and a triangle.

. . . Each is indispensable to the other . . . neither could stand without the other. Romeo, as you will see, will do all the work and Juliet cuddle alongside to support and exalt him. . . . The storm-strains on the harmonious pair will be resolved into one another and be tuned into a pull on the iron straps built deep into the stone foundation . . .

*"Romeo and Juliet" Windmill Tower*

To be run in concrete same as a grain elevator is constructed. Projecting slab at top is lighting fixture to illuminate the walls. Building set back so overhang covers only own ground-space.

This is a design for an urban hotel without interior corridors, regular windows on the street, or stores below to add to congestion and deprive the hotel of its best asset: the comfort and entertainment of its guests. . . . The structure is as completely organic as we can make it, weighing about one-tenth what skyscrapers of the Rockefeller Center type weigh, stabilized at this great height by a single feature . . . the impressive mass of an adequate air-conditioning intake and exhaust, to which all parts of the great hotel have direct access.

Because the building is in the form of an open court, the center of this space will be in bright light and become a large water basin over the service features below. . . . In plan the life of the hotel is in the patio. By this simple means, its to-and-fro, ordinarily humdrum, is here dramatized and made interesting in spite of itself.

Should any guest prefer to turn from the dazzling beauty of this interior to view the street, the view is available by openings provided for that purpose.

If our cities are to continue habitable, something like this turning inward, over ample parking facilities, all avoiding competition with surrounding mercantile establishments, introducing an element of repose and real harmony into building, is absolutely necessary.

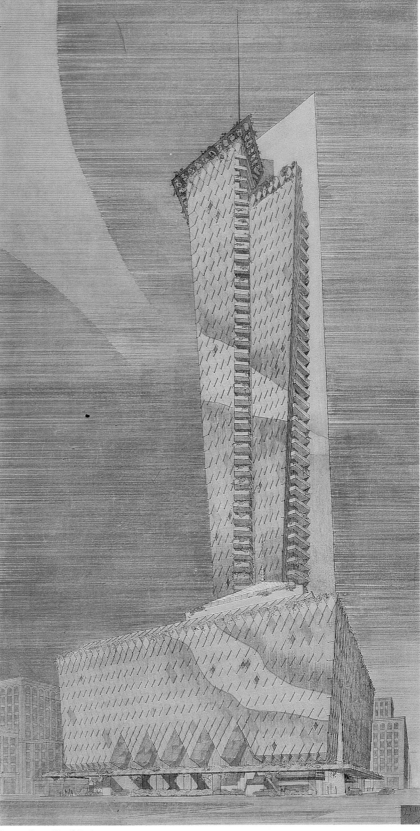

*Rogers Lacy Hotel Project*

*Rogers Lacy Hotel Project*

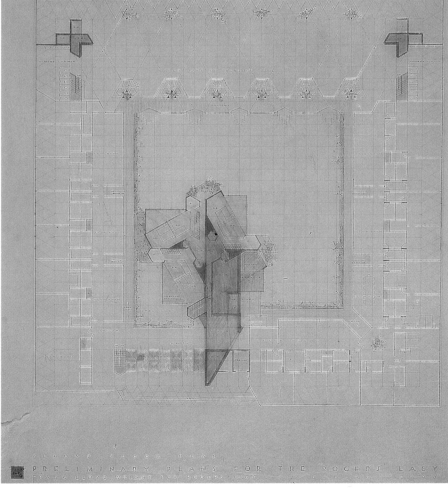

*Rogers Lacy Hotel Project*

*Rogers Lacy Hotel Project*

*California House Project*

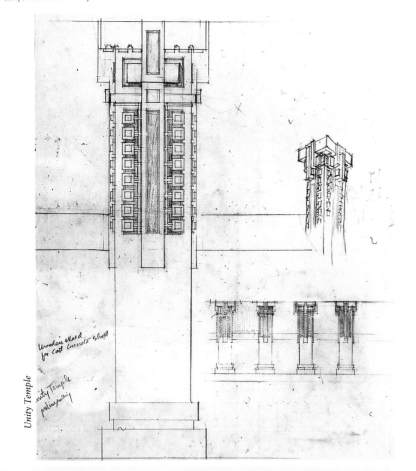

Aesthetically concrete has neither song nor any story. Nor is it easy to see in this conglomerate, in this mud pie, a high aesthetic property, because in itself it is amalgam, aggregate compound. And cement, the binding medium, is characterless.

But, mainly, concrete is still a mass material taking form from moulds, erroneously called "forms." The material of which the moulds themselves are made will, therefore, modify the shape the concrete naturally takes, if indeed it does not wholly determine it.

Unity Temple at Oak Park was entirely cast in wooden boxes, ornamentation and all. . . . The whole is a great casting articulated in sections according to the masses of concrete that could safely be made to withstand changes of temperature in a severe climate.

*Brown House*

First block house.

What about the concrete block? It was the cheapest (and ugliest) thing in the building world. It lived mostly in the architectural gutter as an imitation of rock-faced stone. Why not see what could be done with that gutter rat? Steel rods cast inside the joints of the blocks themselves and the whole brought into some broad, practical scheme of general treatment, why would it not be fit for a new phase of our modern architecture? It might be permanent, noble, beautiful.

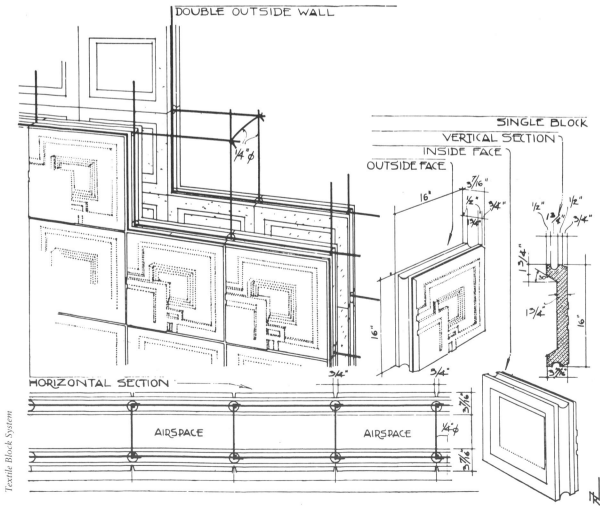

*Textile Block System*

Concrete is a plastic material—susceptible to the impress of imagination. I saw a kind of weaving coming out of it.

*"La Miniatura" (Alice Millard House)*

*Storer House*

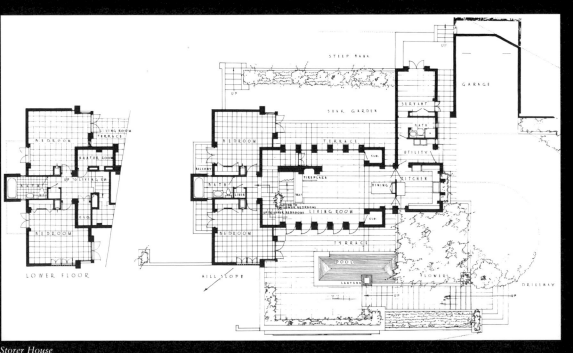

Lightness and strength! Steel the spider spinning a web within the cheap, molded material and wedded to it by pouring an inner core of cement after the blocks were set up.

*Storer House*

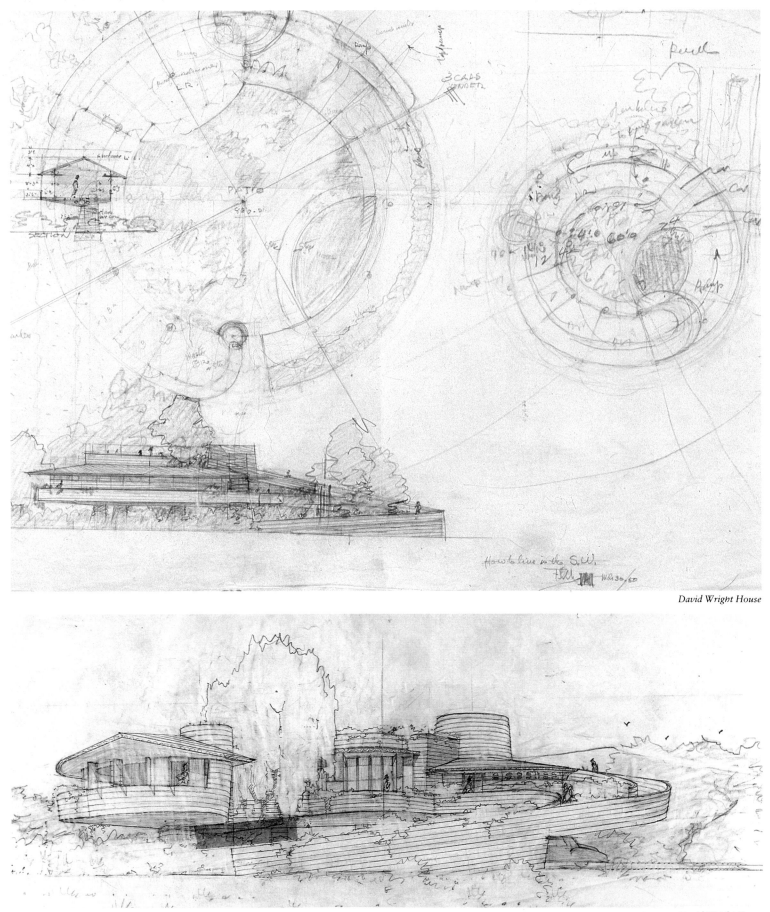

*David Wright House*

*David Wright House*

*David Wright House*

*Kalil House*

Here then, within moderate means for the free man of our democracy, with some intelligence and by his own energy, comes a natural house designed in accordance with the principles of organic architecture. A house that may be put to work in our society and give us an architecture for "housing" which is becoming to a free society because, though standardized fully, it yet establishes the democratic ideal of variety—the sovereignty of the individual.

→

The Usonian Automatic house is built of shells made up of precast concrete blocks, 1′0″ × 2′0″. All edges of the blocks, having a semi-circular groove, admit the steel rods.

Grooved as they are on their edges, they can be set up with small steel horizontal and vertical reinforcing rods, by the owners themselves, each course being grouted (poured) as it is laid upon the one beneath; the rods meantime projecting above for the next course.

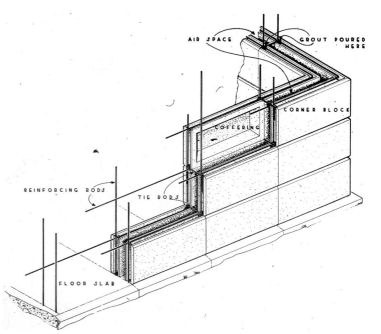

*Usonian Automatic System*

*Johnson Research Tower*

New life, new purposes and possibilities were given to both cement and steel when the coefficient of expansion and contraction was found to be the same in each. A new world was then and there opened to the architect.

→

By way of a natural use of steel in tension, weight in this building appears to lift and float in light and air; miraculous light dendriforms standing up against the sky take on integral character, plastic units of a plastic building construction, emphasizing space instead of standing in the way as mere inserts for support.

*Johnson Administration Building*

*Larkin Administration Building*

Sheet Metal: Membranes of metal to be fed to the machine at its best. Machine made material for rolling, cutting, stamping, folding metal sheets. . . . It is possible that our modern world will be shaped accordingly. For that an entirely new grammar is necessary.

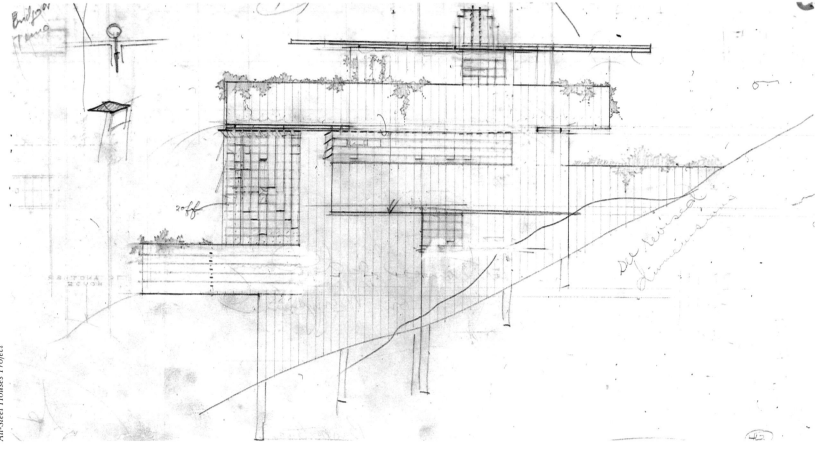

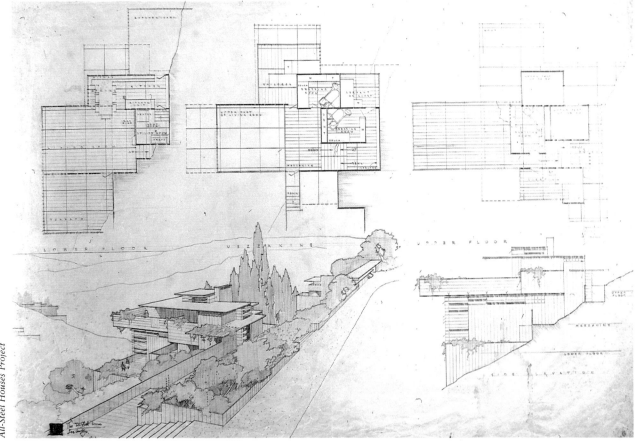

Sheet metal structure—studio living room—cantilever mezzanine type for dwelling—Unit System

Furnished except movables

One section used throughout—interpenetrated with casting of vermiculite or concrete.

Windows and doors same sheet wall section.

Wardrobes and stationary furniture same.

Sheet metal section perforated for glass insertion for windows.

Doors, walls, ceilings, same.

Appurtenance systems all independent of structure—shop fabricated.

No bolts—screws—or mechanical fastenings—

No field labor except assembly and pouring of concrete.

←

Susceptible of great variety of arrangement, the 101 houses all different.

*Anne Pfeiffer Chapel, Florida Southern College*

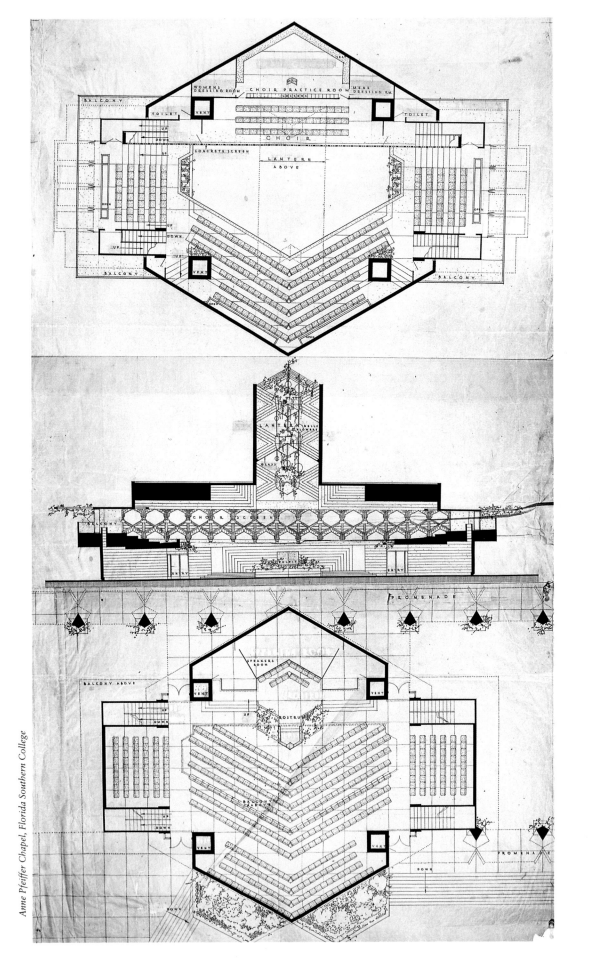

*Anne Pfeiffer Chapel, Florida Southern College*

Here we have reinforced concrete, a new dispensation. A new medium for the new world of thought and feeling that seems ideal: a new world that must follow freedom from the imprisonment in the abstract in which tradition binds us. Democracy means liberation from those abstractions, and therefore life, more abundantly in the concrete. It happens to be so literally, for concrete combined with steel strands will probably become the physical body of the modern civilized world.

*"Fallingwater" (Edgar J. Kaufmann House)*

*Self-Service Garage Project*

Each building will have a grammar of its own, true to materials, as in the new grammar of Fallingwater, my first dwelling in reinforced concrete.

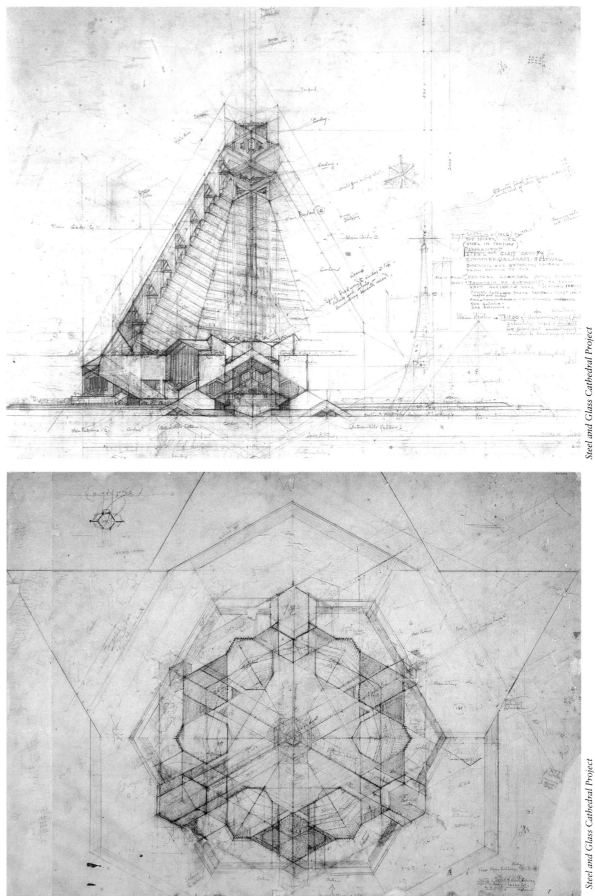

In the steel and glass buildings I have designed, there are no walls, only wall-screens. The method of the cantilever in concrete and steel yields best to suspended screens or shells in place of outer walls; all may be shop-fabricated. The spider web is a good inspiration for steel construction.

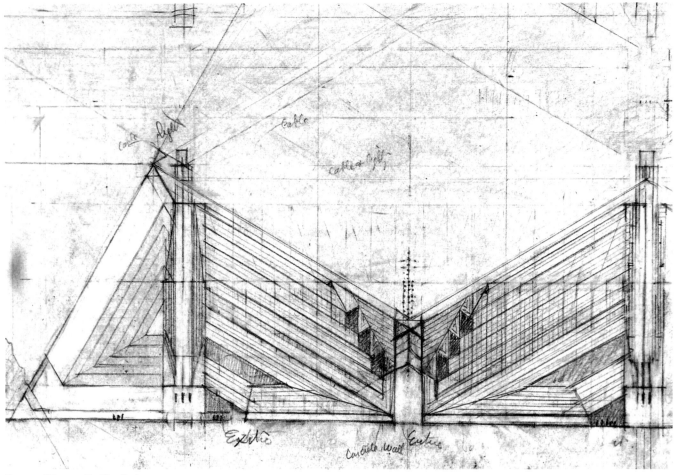

*Century of Progress Pavilion Project*

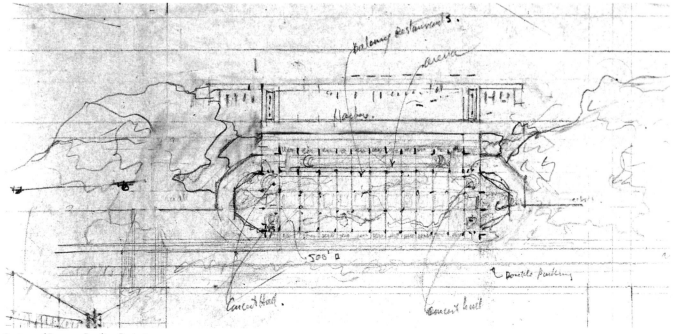

*Century of Progress Pavilion Project*

. . . A canopy would be anchored by steel cables to the outer series of pylons. Weave main and minor and intermediate cables, a network to support transparent glass substitutes, and thus make an architectural canopy more beautiful and more vast than any ever seen. The canopy could rise five hundred feet at the pylons, to fall between them to one hundred and fifty feet above the park. The fabric should fall at the sides as a screen to close the space against wind. Rain would wash the roof spaces or they could be flushed from the pylon tops as fountains, the water spouting through openings at the low points of the canopy into fountain basins, features of the lagoons that would wind and thread their way beneath the canopy through the greenery of the park.

All trees, foliage and waterways could be joined by moving walkways reaching individual plots allotted to exhibitors. . . . The old fair spirit, exciting as of old—but made free to excite the sophisticated modern ego once more by great spans and wondrous spinning.

COUNTRY CLUB FOR HUNTINGTON HARTFORD        HOLLYWOOD
FRANK LLOYD WRIGHT · ARCHITECT

*Huntington Hartford Play Resort and Sports Club Project*

*Twin Cantilevered Bridges Project*

← A good building is the greatest of poems when it is organic architecture. The building faces and is reality and serves while it releases life; daily life is better worth living and all the necessities are happier because of useful living in a building none the less poetry, but more truly so. Every great architect is—necessarily—a great poet.

↑ Steel is most economical in tension; the steel strand is a marvel, let us say, as compared with anything the ancients knew; a miracle of strength for its weight and cost. We have found now how to combine it with a mass material, concrete, which has great strength in compression.

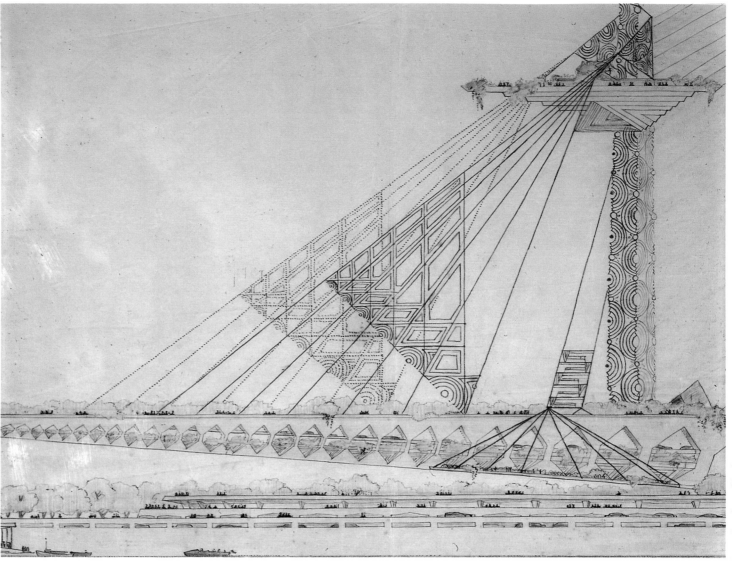

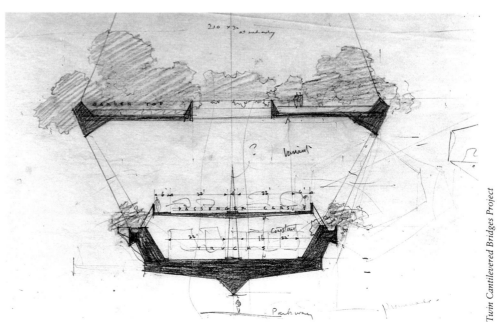

*Twin Cantilevered Bridges Project*

Now ductile, tensile, dense to any degree, uniform and calculable to any standard, steel is a known quantity to be dealt with mathematically to a certainty to the last pound: a miracle of strength to be counted upon.

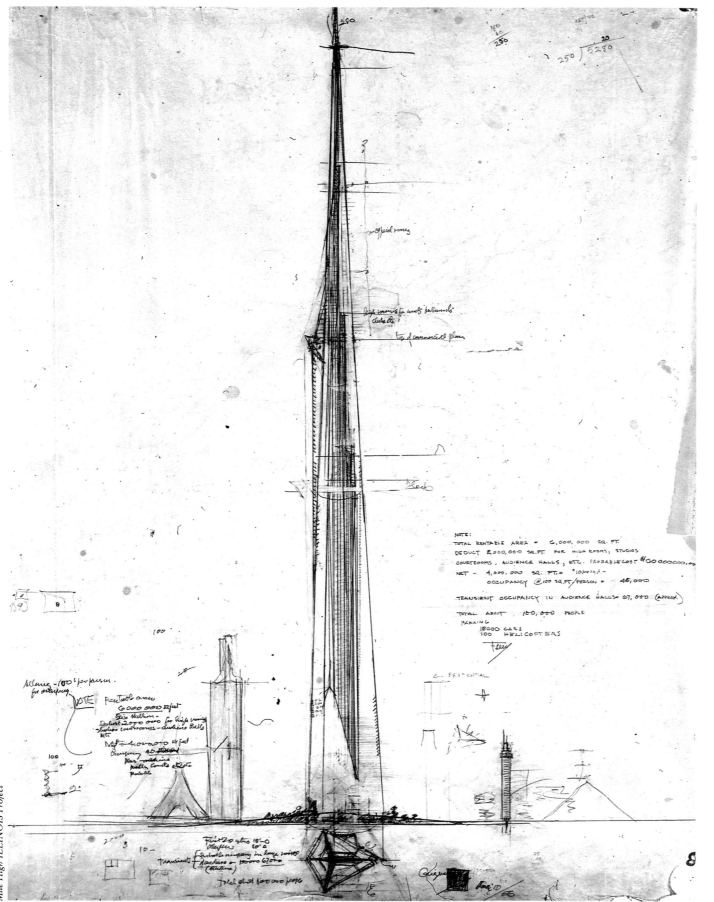

*Mile High ILLINOIS Project*

Note: Total rentable area =
  6,000,000 sq. ft.
deduct 2,000,000 sq. ft. for high
  rooms, studios, courtrooms
  audience halls, etc.
net 4,000,000 sq. ft.
occupancy @ 100 sq. ft./person
  45,000
transient occupancy in audience
  halls = 67,000 approx.
total about 100,000 people
$10 per sq. ft. $60,000,000.00
parking 15,000 cars
100 helicopters

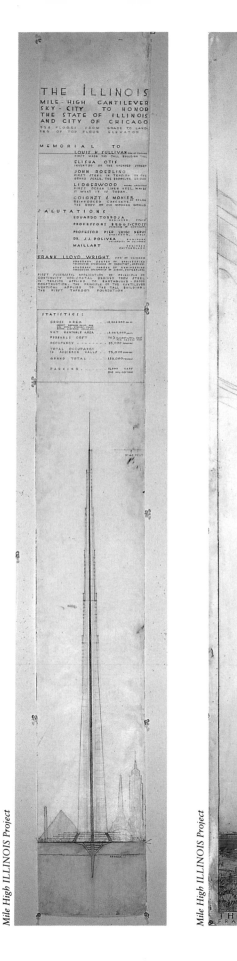

*Mile High ILLINOIS Project*

*Mile High ILLINOIS Project*

Of all forms of upright structure, the most stable is the tripod: pressures upon any side immediately resisted by the other two. For general stability at great height this form of the ILLINOIS is planned to employ the new principles of cantilever—steel in suspension—as in the Imperial Hotel, Tokyo, the Johnson Heliolaboratory at Racine, Wisconsin, and the Price Tower at Bartlesville, Oklahoma.

The exterior wall screens are suspended from the edges of the rigid upright steel cores—cores buried in light-weight concrete: this building thus designed from the inside outward instead of the dated steel-framed construction from outside inward.

For instance, the support of the outer walls and sixteen feet of the outer area of the floors is pendent, and the science of continuity is employed everywhere else.

Excepting the vertical elevator enclosures, which issue from the sloping sides of the tripod, all exterior surface-features of this structure and certain outer areas of the floors are suspended by steel strands from the sloping corners of the core as already described. Outer glass surfaces are set back four feet under the metal parapets to avoid glare of glass and afford a human sense of protection at such enormous heights as characterize the ILLINOIS SKY-CITY.

Elevator transit is by atomic power; especially designed elevators. . . . A group of 76 tandem-cab elevators five units high begin to load where the escalators leave off at the fifth floor.

The ILLINOIS employs the now proved system of "tap-root" foundation sloping to hard-pan or bedrock. . . . Throughout this light-weight tensilized structure, because of the integral character of all members, loads are in equilibrium at all points, doing away with oscillation. . . . A rapier, with handle the breadth of the hand, set firmly into the ground, blade upright, as a simile, indicates the general idea of the ILLINOIS five times the height of the highest structure in the world.

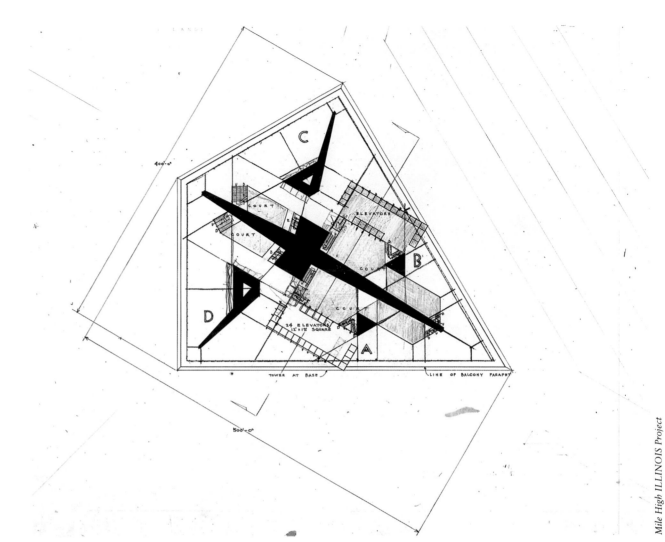

*Mile High ILLINOIS Project*

The ILLINOIS is divided into four parts, and is reached at four points by four four-lane approaches. Fountain features and green-planted parterres are thus related to the tripod entrances, each independent of the other.

By new products of technology and increased inventive ingenuity in applying them to building-construction many superlative new space-forms have already come alive: and because of them, more continually in sight. . . . But more important, modern building becomes the solid creative art which the poetic principle can release and develop. Noble, vital, exuberant forms are already here. Democracy awakes to a more spiritual expression. Indigenous culture will now awaken.

# BUILDING FOR DEMOCRACY

I declare, the time is here for architecture to recognize its own nature, to realize the fact that it is out of life itself for life as it is now lived, a humane and therefore an intensely human thing; it must again become the most human of all expressions of human nature

I have always wanted to build for the man of today, build his tomorrow in, organic to his own Time and his Place as modern Man.

This upshoot of indigenous art is already dedicated to our democracy: alive none too soon, organic expression of modern life square with our forefathers' faith in man as Man. Sovereignty of the individual now stems true as the core of indigenous culture in the arts and architecture.

That is why I have always referred to this as the architecture of democracy: the freedom of the individual becomes the motive for society and government.

To Americans thus came natural, free building. For mankind *THE IDEAL* of man free, therefore his own building humanistic. Both of these freedoms I understood then as now to be basic to all our modern art, parallel to the *IDEA* by which we live and have our being as people. This is the meaning of democracy.

There is no such thing as creative except by the individual. Humanity, especially on a democratic basis, lives only by virtue of individuality. The whole endeavor, the whole effort of our education and our government, should be to discover first—then cherish, use and protect the individual.

*Broadacre City Project*

Architectural features of true democratic ground-freedom would rise naturally from topography; which means that buildings would all take on the nature and character of the ground on which in endless variety they would stand and be component of.

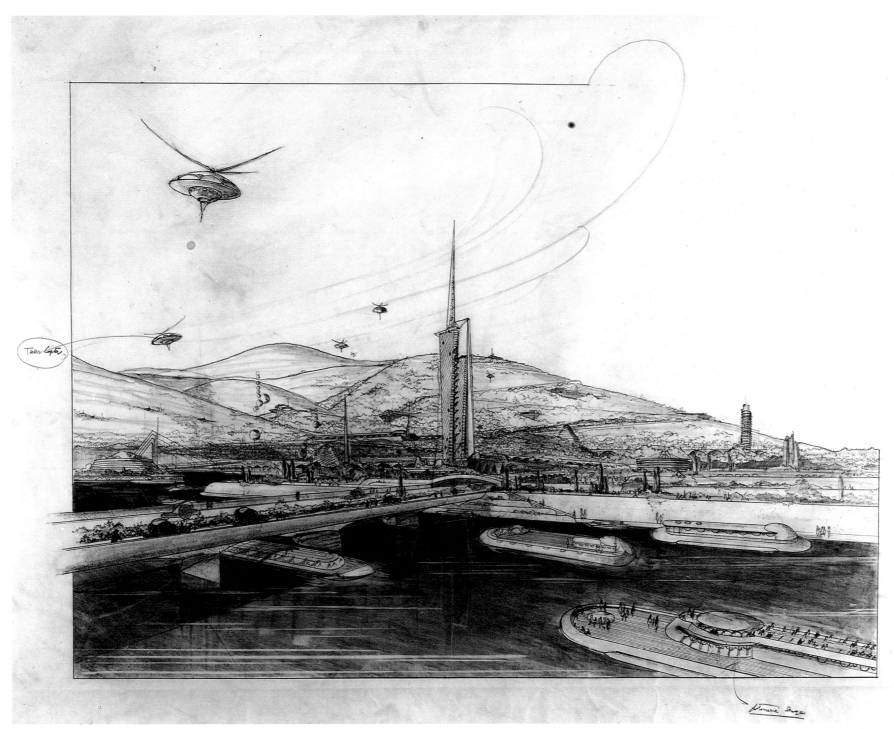

*Broadacre City Project*

To see where the ground leaves off and the building begins
would require careful attention.

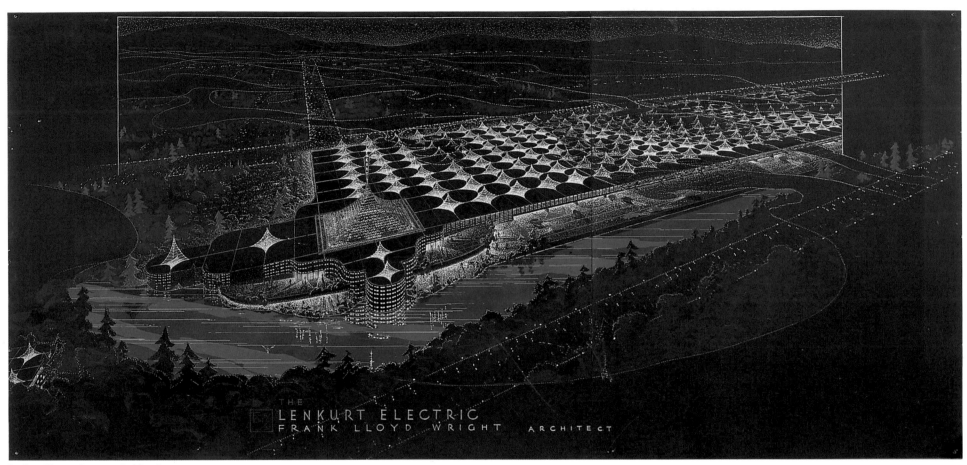

*Lenkurt Electric Company Building Project*

Now the factory comes to our country-wide city that is a nation. But the factory is already so well organized, built, and managed in our country that it needs less redesigning than any other enterprise we have; but it needs the ground free; ground available for factory decentralization but also ground free to factory workers.

→
I believe a remarkably fine thing is going to be industry's contribution to American culture. The business world can do most after the American dwelling . . .

*Lenkurt Electric Company Building Project*

Unified Farm Project Model

Agronomy, the equal of industrialism or superior, is the gifted source of our national culture—even now—if you take a fair view of our country.

This composite farm-building would be made up of assembled prefabricated units. . . . The whole establishment would be good architecture. Good to look at. Emancipation for the life of the farmer. As such the whole farm-unit could well be delivered to the farmers at low cost by machine production intelligently expanded and standardized. For the first time organic architecture would become his own, serving him by way of the best brains utilized to simplify and make his life more dignified and his whole family effective help. Their life would become attractive not only to themselves but to the new city itself, a feature of a true modern agronomy countrywide.

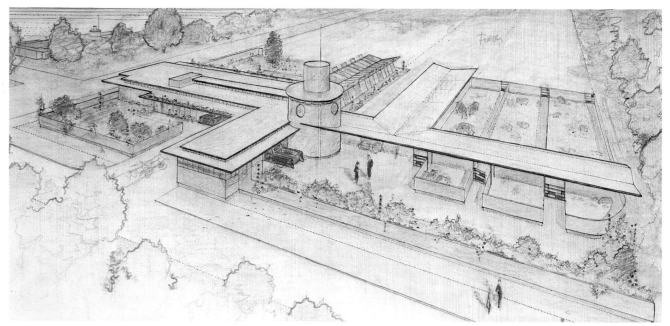

Unified Farm Project

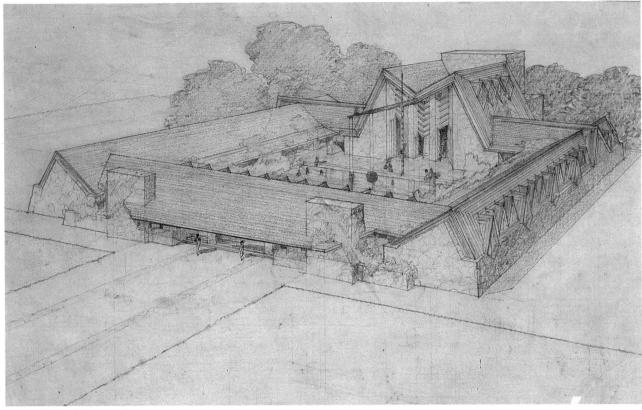

*Rosenwald School Project*

For the schools more excellent teachers. Smaller and smaller flocks! Decentralization a natural aim in the direction of their education. Because the common school period ending in high school seems to be the most constructive period in education.

When Dr. Ludd M. Spivey, the presidential good-genius of Florida Southern College, flew North to Taliesin, he came with the express and avowed purpose of giving the United States at least one example of a college wherein life was to have the advantages of modern science and art in actual building construction. He said he wanted me as much for my Philosophy as for my Architecture. I assured him they were inseparable.

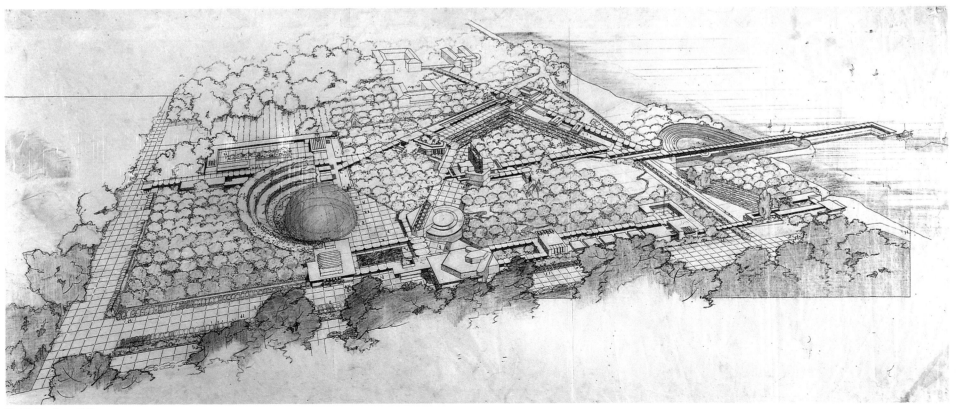

*Florida Southern College*

*Florida Southern College*

The buildings do not crowd each other, but each has its own stretch of esplanade and intervening trees.

You will see in these buildings now standing at Florida Southern College the sentiment of a true educational saga along the cultural lines of an indigenous Architecture for our own country.

*Baird House*

The true center (the only centralization allowable) in Usonian democracy, is the individual Usonian home. In that we have the nuclear building which we must learn how to build. Integration is vitally necessary. Differentiation, too, is just as necessary. Free individual choice is what the home should especially cherish, free choice eventually based upon a greater range of possible freedom.

*Christian Science Church Project*

Traditional church forms, like so many traditions now, must die
in all minor forms in order that Tradition in great form may live!
To understand this truth is to understand the changing growth that
is already due to the idea of democracy, and to make way for the
return of worship to the life of the citizen as well as for the uplift
and integrity the nation requires to endure. As Walt Whitman and
Emerson and Thomas Jefferson prophesied.

*Dallas Theatre Center*

Wherever a phase of Nature will have been raised by society to the level of greater Nature there we will find the Theater and find the people themselves owner and producer. Theater would be radical, arousing, inspiring, challenging popular emotion, presenting native problems. Human strength and aspiration would go there for inspiration.

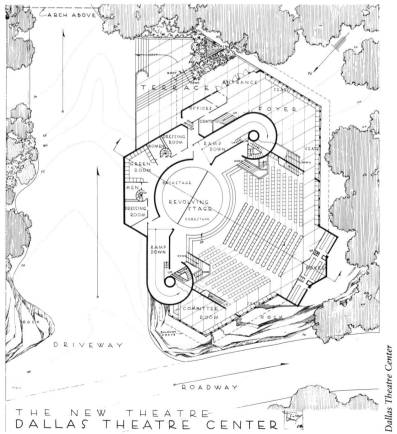

THE NEW THEATRE
DALLAS THEATRE CENTER

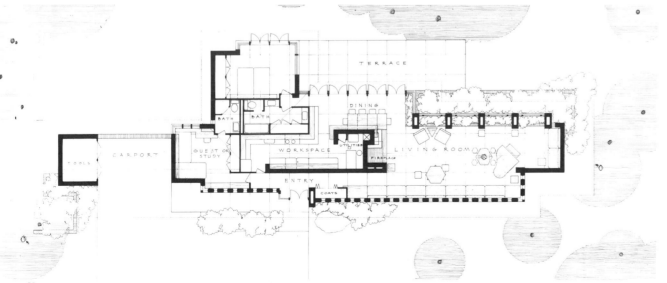

With organic architecture, man is a noble feature of his own ground, integral as trees, the sculptor-streams, and the ribs of rocks that are our hills.

CRYSTAL HEIGHTS WASHINGTON DC FRANK LLOYD WRIGHT ARCHITECT
FOR ROY S THURMAN

A tall building may be very beautiful, economical and desirable in itself—provided always that it is in no way interference with what lives below, but looking further ahead than the end of landlord's ruse—by inhabiting a small green park. That park is humane now. The skyscraper is no longer sane unless in free green space.

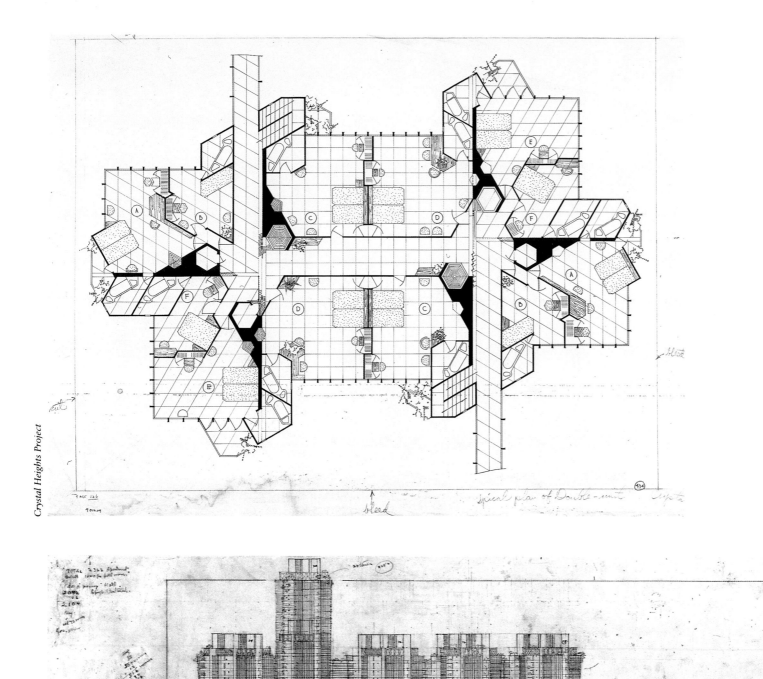

Crystal Heights Project

Crystal Heights Project

CONNECTICUT AVENUE ELEVATION          SCALE 1" = 22' 0"

*Cloverleaf Housing Project*

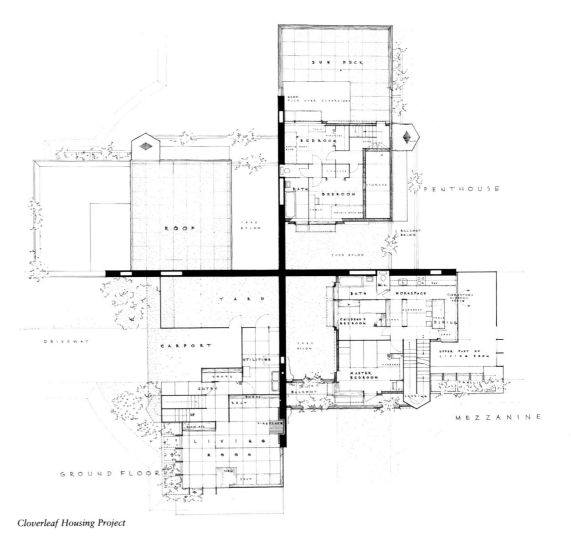

Every man's home his "castle"! No, every man's home his sphere in space—his appropriate place to live in spaciousness. On his own sunlit sward or in wood or strand enhancing all other homes. No less but more than ever this manly home a refuge for the expanding spirit of man the individual.

*Cloverleaf Housing Project*

*Golden Beacon Project*

Such tall buildings would stand in iridescence of vivid color in the landscape, set up in spacious blossoming grounds in the midst of a neighborhood of varied activities all similarly independent—*each presentable to all!*

Within the illustration:

REGIONAL DEVELOPMENT WITH HIGHWAYS AND PARK SYSTEMS
PROPOSED BY THE FRANK LLOYD WRIGHT FOUNDATION

*Butterfly Bridge Project*

. . . A standardized unit system cantilever bridge, staunch and
easy to repeat any number of times anywhere—either independent
of shop fabrication or employing it. The type is called the Butterfly
because the wingspread of the spans concentrates the load upon a
deep central girder economical up to spans of 200 ft. The low
sweeping arches become an asset to any landscape.

*Marin County Fair Project*

    The community center would mean more because it would be
salient feature of every countryside development of the county,
wherever the county seat might be. The civic center would always
be an attractive automobile objective—perhaps situated just off
some major highway in interesting landscape—noble and
inspiring.

A simple commodious arrangement for her official family: the senate, the assembly, the supreme court and the chief executive suites—all provided conveniently with ample offices, committee rooms, lounges, refectory and a great hall for the people in which the history of the state would be memorialized. . . . Stone, copper, plastics, employed in the great ferro-concrete system of construction that now constitutes the twentieth century body of our world.

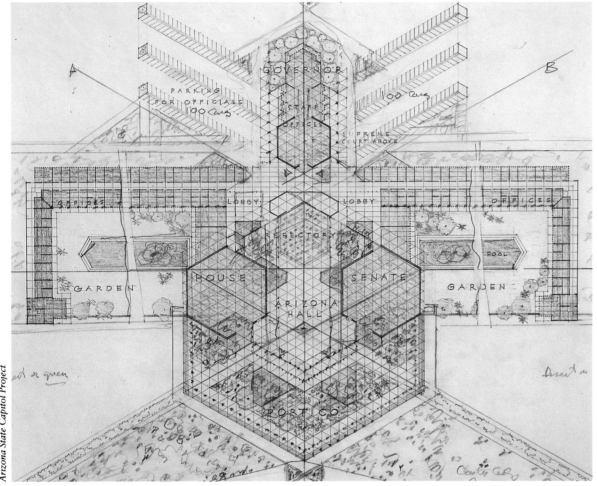

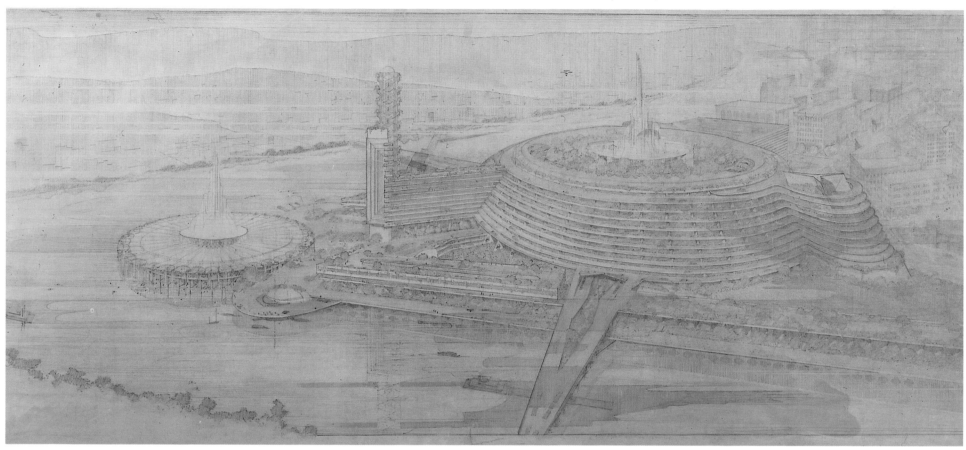

*Pittsburgh Point Civic Center Project*

The community center would be the great common club of clubs, avoiding commonplace elegance and overcoming popular prejudice of town partisanship. The community center, liberal and inspiring, would be a general culture-factor because it would be an entertainment center. The art gallery a popular rendezvous, not so much a museum; a "morgue" no longer.

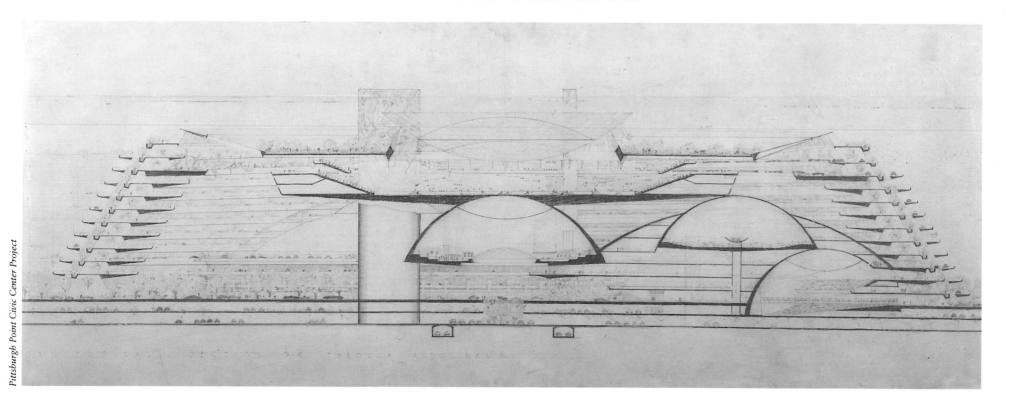

The community center thus would catch, retain, and express the best thought of which growing American democracy is capable.

*Bazett House*

Buildings may be so economized by intelligent standardizing that "home" may now be open to beautiful environment and be designed to broaden the life of the individual family, making site and building a unit.

*Wieland Motel Project*

Each motel, now as hotel, would probably be a group of small units conveniently related to a larger unit comprising public services—separate rooms for the use of all guests, as already seen in the better planned motel.

VIEW FROM NORTH
HOUSE FOR MR. AND MRS. GERALD B. TONKENS
CINCINNATI, OHIO
FRANK LLOYD WRIGHT ARCHITECT

*Tonkens House*

Then, when every man, woman and child may put his feet on his own acre and every unborn child finds his acre wating for him when he is born—then, by way of organic education, organic architecture becomes the greatest servant of man in modern times.

A rational, important change in civilization is possible because architecture for the individual becomes not only reasonable but is the only possible architecture. So the architecture of democracy is here.

## ⌘. IN CONCLUSION

The workings of principle in the direction of integral order is your only safe precedent, now or ever.

I am here to assure you that the circumference of architecture is changing with astonishing rapidity but that its center remains unchanged, the human heart.

According to our strength of character and our clarity of vision, we will endure, we will succeed, we will have contributed something to make life where we were and as we lived it better, brighter, and more beautiful.

PART TWO
COMMENTARIES

# FRANK LLOYD WRIGHT IN 1893:
## THE CHICAGO CONTEXT
*Jack Quinan*

Early in 1893 Louis Sullivan discovered that his chief draftsman, Frank Lloyd Wright, had been designing houses for clients independently of the Adler and Sullivan firm. Sullivan confronted Wright about the matter, asserting that such activity detracted from Wright's commitment to the firm. Wright, according to his own account of the incident,[1] had mixed feelings: he was aware of having deceived Sullivan but he resented the angry accusation. When Sullivan refused to relinquish the deed to Wright's home in Oak Park, Wright quit the firm and proceeded to establish his own architectural practice. Thus began the career of America's most renowned architect.

Frank Lloyd Wright's architectural achievement has been the subject of extensive scholarly interest over the past fifty years, an interest that has been confined (except for an ongoing public preoccupation with Wright's personal life) to the evolution of his architecture. Henry-Russell Hitchcock set the tone in *In the Nature of Materials* (1942), which traces the evolution of Wright's work, building by building, with reference to little else but Louis Sullivan. Grant Manson followed Hitchcock's example in his more narrowly focused *Frank Lloyd Wright to 1910: The First Golden Age* (1958); Sullivan is again discussed, and Japanese architecture and the Froebel method are introduced as significant formative influences. Vincent Scully has emphasized Wright's relationship to history, especially indigenous Native American sources and the work of Bruce Price, H. H. Richardson, and McKim, Mead and White.[2] Recently historians have begun to examine Wright's later work.

Yet relatively little attention has been given to the larger sociocultural context of Wright's work. Why? Probably in part because Wright's architecture is so obviously different from that of his peers, and in greater part because he took pains in his writings and public appearances to isolate his work from and oppose it to the dominant cultural and artistic forces of his time. In this dramatic opposition of his work to that of his American contemporaries much has been simplified and even lost. Wright was, after all, a man of his times, and one measure of his achievement is his success in engaging, and even embodying, what was significant about those times.

Frank Lloyd Wright was born into a tumultuous period of American history. The Civil War had barely ended, and the assassination of Abraham Lincoln, Reconstruction, and the impeachment of Andrew Johnson had served to prolong the nation's agony. Thanks to weak presidents, widespread corruption in government, nationwide economic depressions in

Jack Quinan studied at Brown University and Dartmouth College, taking his M.A. and Ph.D. degrees at Brown. He is Associate Professor of Architectural History at the State University of New York at Buffalo. He has published many articles on Frank Lloyd Wright's architecture, with a focus on buildings in New York State, and is currently preparing a book on Wright's Larkin Administration Building for the MIT Press.

1873 and 1893, and immense social problems brought on by immigration, industrialization, and the rapid growth of cities, a mood of uncertainty permeated the land. There were parallel uncertainties in Wright's boyhood home, caused by his father's inability to hold a job, the family's frequent moves to new towns, and the resulting tensions between his parents, who divorced in 1885.[3]

America's underlying trepidation was masked, however, by the free-wheeling, headlong nature of business and industry, where personal fortunes of mythic proportions were attained in a relatively short time by men like Andrew Carnegie, J. P. Morgan, Henry Clay Frick, Cornelius Vanderbilt, and John D. Rockefeller. Historians have characterized this as the "Age of Enterprise," the "Age of Energy," the "Age of Urbanization," the "Age of the Moguls," and the "Age of the Robber Barons." Wright, in his inventiveness, his dependency on industrial developments, his personal flamboyance, and, above all, his extraordinary energy, embodies many of the leading characteristics of this period.

Industrialism was the dominant force in post–Civil War America. Prior to the war the United States had trailed behind England and France in industrial production, but in the decades following the war it emerged as the world's leading industrial nation. Although the war itself had stimulated the production of arms and supplies and the development of modern transportation systems, the nation's industrial preeminence was due primarily to its vast natural resources, its ample supply of immigrant laborers, the traditional American work ethic, and the free enterprise system. The principal industries were those fundamental to the development of an advanced machine technology: the mining of such raw materials as coal, iron, and oil; the development of railroads, which carried materials to manufacturers and goods to users; and the manufacturing industries themselves. Using assembly-line production methods, steam and electrical power, and iron and steel machines and machine tools, these industries produced a seemingly unlimited variety of products, many of which—for example, typewriters, barbed wire, repeating rifles, and locomotives—had the capacity to significantly transform aspects of American life.

The industrial boom of the later 1800s had a particularly strong impact upon architecture. In bringing together materials and people for the processes of manufacturing and merchandising, industrialism in effect *created* the modern city, an aggregate of tall office buildings, hotels, apartment houses, transportation centers, factories, and warehouses threaded with tenements and surrounded by suburban neighborhoods. Historians of architecture have identified the metal-framed tall office building as the quintessential architectural achievement of the industrial age in America, and it is generally agreed that most of the significant developments in the evolution of the tall office building occurred in Chicago.

The evolution of the metal-framed office building has been described by Carl Condit, Sigfried Giedion, William Jordy, and others.[4] The story begins with the great Chicago fire of 1871, proceeds tentatively forward with the early buildings of William LeBaron Jenney, Adler and Sullivan, and Burnham and Root around 1879–1884, is momentarily sidetracked by the monumental presence of H. H. Richardson's Marshall Field Store of 1885, and reaches a culmination with the reconciliation of art and technology in such works as Adler and Sullivan's Wainwright Building of 1890, Burnham and Root's (and Atwood's) Reliance Building of 1890/1894–95, and Holabird and Roche's Marquette Building of 1893.

Although it is well known that Frank Lloyd Wright joined Adler and Sullivan in 1887 and remained with them through their most productive and triumphant years, he has left very little record of what happened during those five and one-half years beyond some office anecdotes, a short character sketch of Dankmar Adler, and a carefully worded, sometimes ambiguous discussion of his relationship with Louis Sullivan.[5] As a result, historians have been left to their own devices in trying to relate the evolution of the tall office building and that of the Prairie House. Wright's interest in the relationship of form and function obviously owes a substantial debt to Sullivan, and it is possible to recognize an echo of the Chicago tall building frame in some of Wright's more skeletalized Prairie houses, but beyond that all is speculation.

Perhaps a more fruitful approach than relating evolutionary building sequences is to choose a fixed point in time to explore some of the leading issues, events, and circumstances that would have concerned a young prospective architect in Chicago at the end of the nineteenth century. I have chosen 1893 because it was the year that Wright broke with Sullivan and began the practice that would alter the course of architecture in both America and Europe far into the twentieth century. It was also the year of the World's Columbian Exposition in Chicago, an event of no small consequence to Wright and to the history of American architecture. From the densely woven fabric of American culture in the 1890s, I have chosen three subjects of particular relevance to architecture—industrialism, style, and the nature of architectural practice—as central to an inquiry into the nature of Wright's activities during those first years in Chicago.

## INDUSTRIALISM

The significance of the role of industrial technology cannot be overstated. Anyone born during the 1860s, as Wright was, was exposed in his formative years to constant innovation, invention, and change. Steam engines, electrical motors, flush toilets, gas stoves, telegraphs, telephones, electric lights, cameras, trolleys, phonographs, and innumerable other devices appeared in rapid succession, bewildering to some, perhaps, but exciting to people of energy and vision. Wright's 1901 essay "The Art and Craft of the Machine"[6] is his earliest public declaration of acceptance of these devices, but the collective evidence of his entire career—from the chain trusses of his Oak Park studio (1895) to the bold use of reinforced concrete in the Guggenheim Museum of the 1950s—suggest that his openly experimental attitude toward the materials and technologies of architecture originated during the 1880s and 1890s.

As a draftsman in one of America's leading architectural firms, Wright would have been exposed to the latest innovations in building technology as a matter of course. In addition to the metal frame, there were important developments in foundations, cladding, glazing, windbracing, fireproofing, waterproofing, electrical wiring, plumbing, heating and ventilation, elevators, and so forth, many of which had a direct impact on design considerations. I have selected two examples to indicate something of the breadth of Wright's exposure to new technology during his five and one-half years with Adler and Sullivan.

First, glass. The introduction of the metal frame during the nineteenth century generated a need for sheets of glass that were substantially larger than could be produced by traditional glass-blowing methods. Plate glass was highly desirable for merchandising display windows on city streets and for office windows that would admit generous amounts of natural light, especially during the years before electric lighting became commonly available. The development of modern plate glass began in 1860 when it was discovered that a purer glass could be attained by firing the necessary ingredients in a Siemans regenerative gas-fired furnace. The optimum chemical composition for the most durable glass was determined by scientific investigation in 1875, and during the succeeding decades several rolled-plate processes for producing plate glass were in operation in the United States.

It is instructive to compare such early Adler and Sullivan works as the Revell Building (1881–83), the Ryerson Building (1884), and the Troescher Building (1884), in which the metal-framed bays are filled with three-abreast sash-type windows of equal widths, with buildings from the 1890s such as the Prudential Building in Buffalo, whose street-level bays are spanned with a single plate of glass ten feet square, or the Stock Exchange Building in Chicago (1893–94), whose "Chicago Window," a plate glass element measuring at least five feet square flanked by two sash-type side lights, is repeated through twelve stories. In keeping with this developing technology, Wright used unusually large square panes of window glass in his first independent commission, the William Winslow House of 1893, at a time when his Eastern contemporaries were continuing to use grids of small panes for picturesque (Shingle style) and historical (Colonial Revival) reasons. By the 1900s Wright was using a version of the "Chicago Window" in some of his Prairie houses. "Chicago Windows" also appear on the long sides of the Larkin Administration Building in Buffalo of 1903–6, whose entrance doors of glass in a metal frame surrounded by more glass have since become a commonplace feature of commercial architecture.

Wright continued to press the technology of glass toward new limits in his post-Prairie years. His National Life Insurance Company project of 1924 shares with Mies van der Rohe's more hypothetical glazed projects of about the same time the claim to being the first crystalline skyscraper. As late as 1946, in his seventy-ninth year, Wright continued his relentless pursuit of new uses for glass in architecture in his plan for the Rogers Lacy Hotel in Dallas. For this project he proposed an exterior wall of triangular glass panels two layers thick with an air space between them that was to be filled with glass wool insulation so as to admit a softly diffused light.[7]

Next, heating and ventilation technology, which underwent a rapid transformation during Wright's years with Adler and Sullivan. During the 1870s and 1880s office buildings were usually ventilated by the simple process of opening and closing windows, but theaters and other buildings with unusually large interior spaces presented special ventilation problems that necessitated technological advances. E. G. Lind's Peabody Institute Library in Baltimore (1875–78), for instance, contained a handsome skylight hall surrounded by five tiers of cast-iron book-bearing balconies;[8] during the summer months the books in the highest tiers were sometimes damaged by excessive heat.

On the strength of a number of small theater designs and remodelings in the early 1880s, Adler and Sullivan won the competition for the Auditorium Building in 1885, a combination hotel and office building that was to contain a 4,000-seat opera house of such beauty and acoustical perfection that Chicago would gain recognition as a major center for music in North America. Dankmar Adler described his solution to the problems of heating and ventilation in the *Architectural Record*:

Much attention has been paid to the heating, cooling and ventilating apparatus. Fresh air, taken from the top of the building, is forced into the house by a fan having a wheel 10 feet in diameter and 4 feet 6 inches in face. The fresh air comes down through a shaft in which it is subjected to the action of a heavy spray. This, in all seasons of the year, washes from the air much of the soot with which it is charged. In winter, warm brine is used to prevent the shower from freezing. In summer from twelve to twenty tons of ice are used for cooling the shower and with it the air. Salt is mixed with the melting ice to still further lower the temperature. For warming the air in the winter it is carried through steam coils so subdivided and provided with valves that very minute gradations of temperature can be affected. A system of ducts carries the air into the different parts of the auditorium, to the stage and to the various corridors, foyers and dressing-rooms. The general movement of air is from the stage outward and from the ceiling downward. The air is removed from the house by the operation of three disk fans, two of 8 feet diameter and one 6 feet in diameter.[9]

It is safe to assume that Wright, whose only formal university training was in engineering, familiarized himself with Adler's system. In the not too distant future he would be creating heating and ventilating systems of his own.

The heating and ventilation system of Jenney and Mundie's Chicago National Bank of 1900 indicates considerable progress in that technology during the fourteen years following Adler's Auditorium design. Again air was admitted into the building through openings several feet above the roof level. At the basement level the fresh air shaft opened into a chamber from which the air passed in turn through tempering coils, an air-washing spray, an Acme water eliminator (guaranteed to give 98% extraction and to establish an average of 65–75% humidity in the building), an electrically driven blower or blast fan measuring 102 inches in diameter (built by the Chicago firm of Andrews and Johnson), and finally a set of heating coils. Temperature regulation was largely automatic: each main room had a thermostat operated by compressed air connected to mixing dampers at the hot-air and tempered-air chambers. An exhaust-air chamber contained a discharge fan.[10] Jenney and Mundie's system employed electricity and tempering coils rather than brine to prevent freezing, and it offered some humidity control, but there is no indication that it was capable of cooling the air.

Air-conditioning, a combination of cooling and dehumidifying air, was invented by Willis Carrier in Buffalo in 1902, and was first employed in the Sackett-Wilhelms Lithographing and Printing Company in Brooklyn that same year.[11] Early in 1903 Frank Lloyd Wright prepared specifications for the Larkin Administration Building in Buffalo that closely paralleled Jenney and Mundie's system in the Chicago National Bank (a building that Wright asked his Buffalo clients to inspect prior to accepting his plans and specifications),[12] but in addition to an Acme air-purifying and cooling apparatus, Wright called for an electrically driven Carbonic Anhydride refrigerating machine, manufactured by the Kroeschell Ice Machine Company of Chicago, for cooling the air to 50°F in order to reduce its humidity.[13] Although Carrier is universally recognized as the father of air-conditioning, it should be noted that all components of Wright's system for the Larkin Administration Building were manufactured in Chicago. Plainly a significant parallel development in this technology took place in Chicago, and Wright was fully aware of it.

When Wright first arrived in Chicago technological developments and questions of style were separate issues. Historically, new technological developments have frequently acted upon architecture and have enabled architects to express new ideas; but in the unprecedented technological explosion of the post–Civil War period in America so many advances occurred so swiftly that their relationship to style was not immediately apparent to most architects, who clung tenaciously to historical styles.

STYLE

After the realization of the Prairie House around 1900, Wright was quick to dismiss all architectural historicism as mere "sentimentality."[14] Yet his own work from 1887 to 1893 shows considerable derivation from historical styles and from current trends in American architecture. Architectural historians have demonstrated both the latency of Wright's mature architectural principles and his design sources in these early works, but Wright himself has had little to say about them. What, then, was the nature of the discussion of architectural style between 1887 and 1893 in Chicago, and what was Frank Lloyd Wright's relationship to it?

According to recent surveys of American architecture, the sequence of styles that unfolded between 1700 and 1850 gave way after the Civil War to a greater complexity in which several English- and French-derived styles coexisted. Insofar as a development is discernible, it begins with the Victorian and Second Empire modes in the 1860s and 1870s, changes to Queen Anne, Richardson's Romanesque, and the Shingle style in the 1880s, and changes again to Beaux-Arts classicism and the Colonial Revival in the 1890s. New building types, espe-

cially tall office and industrial buildings, designed by architects working in the major East Coast cities borrowed heavily from these historical styles. In Chicago, by contrast, a distinctive functionalist approach emerged.

Wright would not, of course, have perceived this activity as an evolution when he first arrived in Chicago in 1887. His impressions would have been based on what he saw in and around the city and in the architectural offices that employed him, and whatever he may have observed in the architectural periodicals. Witnessing the facility with which his first employer, Joseph Lyman Silsbee, shifted from Victorian to Queen Anne to Colonial Revival, Wright must have questioned the significance of style at the very outset of his career.

He almost certainly read the current literature on architecture, particularly two periodicals, the *American Architect and Building News* (Boston) and the *Inland Architect and News Record* (Chicago), in which journal he published three designs in 1887. In both there was much to interest a prospective young architect. Both carried building news, articles on the architectural profession, news of architecturally related technological developments, historical articles (often serialized from European sources), and engravings and photographs of new buildings. Neither journal discussed theory apart from considerations involved in historicizing style. As might be expected, the *Inland Architect* was concerned less than the *American Architect and Building News* with European issues and events, and more with the ideas and activities of the Chicago School.

Wright's perception of style was subjected to stronger influences when he joined Adler and Sullivan later in 1887. There, through Sullivan, he learned to appreciate the work of H. H. Richardson, the one American architect who was able to break through the welter of styles of the 1860s and 1870s to create an essentially modern approach characterized by a rational organization of building elements, a sensitive consideration of building materials and site, and a restrained and judicious use of ornament. Richardson's importance for Wright may have been heightened by Sullivan's unqualified enthusiasm for him, by the example of three new Richardson buildings in Chicago, and by Richardson's untimely death in 1886. Wright later claimed to have been embarrassed by Sullivan's open adulation of Richardson,[15] but as James O'Gorman has ably demonstrated,[16] Wright learned a great deal from Richardson, whose universal approach to design suited any building type and transcended the specifics of historical style.

Richardson's example notwithstanding, Wright's most important experience was his daily contact with Sullivan over a period of about five and one-half years. Of this substantial apprenticeship we have only the tantalizing glimpses provided in Wright's autobiography and amplified in *Genius and the Mobocracy*. These books describe Sullivan as an arrogant, egotistical genius who was disdainful of all architects but Richardson and John Wellborn Root, and all draftsmen except Wright.[17] Wright acknowledges his closeness to Sullivan but is also relentlessly critical of him, describing Sullivan's essay "Inspiration" as "baying at the moon . . . too sentimental"[18] and questioning Sullivan's praise of Richardson: "The Master brought the manila stretch with the elevation [of the Walker Warehouse] penciled upon it, laid it over my board with the remark, 'Wright, there is the last word in Romanesque.' I puzzled over that remark a lot. What business had he with the Romanesque?"[19]

Wright acknowledges the significance of the Wainwright Building: "This was the great Louis Sullivan monument. His greatest effort. The skyscraper as a new thing beneath the sun, as entity imperfect, but with virtue, individuality, beauty all its own as the tall building was born."[20] But whenever Wright addresses the subject of his relationship with Sullivan he experiences difficulties. He writes, in *An Autobiography*, of a shared sense of rebellion: "And the radical sense of things I had already formed intuitively got great encouragement from him. In fact the very sense of things I had been feeling as rebellion was at work in him."[21] But concerning the debt of his own architecture to Sullivan he is elusive, as in this peculiarly worded paragraph:

He taught me nothing nor did he ever pretend to do so except as he was himself the thing he did and as I could see it for myself. He (the "designing partner") was the educational document in evidence. I learned to read him with certainty just as you shall see him and see me if you are a good reader between the lines. I am sure he would prefer it—that way.[22]

Usually when Wright attempted to acknowledge his debt to Sullivan he was overcome by the need to demonstrate that his own achievement in architecture represented a critical assessment of Sullivan's work. Thus he wrote that Sullivan "seemed unaware of the machine"[23] and was unconcerned with "the nature of materials."[24] Even Wright's best effort to articulate the nature of his debt to Sullivan tells us more about Wright than about Sullivan:

Yes, the significant implication of lieber-meister's gift to me was his practice *"of–the–thing–not–on–it,"* which I recognized and saw most clearly realized in his unique sense of ornament. . . . His sentient integral modulation by imaginative reason proceeding from generals to particulars always inspired me, as it must inspire anyone who can see into it as he drew it. . . . His own soul's philosophy incarnate. Music its only paraphrase and peer.

Nevertheless and because of this music, in course of time I grew eager to go further. . . . I began to ask myself—why not this eternal principle harmonizing any and every building anywhere with environment and for every purpose? Why not the edifice symphonic throughout from footing to coping of the *structure* itself—a harmony like music? . . . I wanted to see, someday, a building continuously plastic from inside to outside, and exterior from outside to inside.[25]

These statements were written with the advantage of hindsight, long after Wright's own architectural vision had matured and his place in history was secure. Even then, decades after the Sullivan years, Wright was unable to write a tribute to Sullivan without glorifying himself. This represents not so much a meanness of spirit on Wright's part; it is instead an indication of the critical and creative resources that Wright had to summon in order to comprehend, absorb, and eventually surpass Sullivan's compelling architectural theory and system of ornament. It is a pity that we do not have more insight into that process.

### WRIGHT AND THE ARCHITECTURAL PROFESSION

Upon leaving Adler and Sullivan, Wright proceeded to establish his own architectural practice along unorthodox lines. Over the years between 1893 and 1912 he rented a series of offices in Chicago, first in the Schiller Building (until 1896) and subsequently in Steinway Hall, the Rookery, the Fine Arts Building, and Orchestra Hall,[26] which were used for meetings with clients and for informal gatherings with friends and colleagues in the profession. However, Wright at first continued to do his drafting at his home in Oak Park, where he had designed the "bootlegged" houses that incurred Sullivan's

wrath.[27] This arrangement seemed to suit Wright, and in 1898 he designed and built a studio-office-library complex alongside his home. Grant Manson described the studio this way:

There was the "Studio," workshop proper, with its carefully planned professional facilities, apart but connected. There were the apprentices, or draftsmen, working more or less *en famille*, taking lunch daily with the patron and his family. It is life in a Continental vein—paternalistic, imperious, strangely alien to American custom. Where did it come from?[28]

Unable to understand why Wright chose to practice this way, Manson concluded that it "defied explanation."[29] He also found Wright's relationship with his professional colleagues in Chicago "interesting," but often "puzzling."[30]

Wright's approach to practice and his relationship to the architectural profession may have been, in some degree, manifestations of his personality, but they were also informed by his experiences and observations of the profession between 1887 and 1893. By the time he arrived in Chicago the architectural profession had undergone an extensive evolution. Beginning with the first professional employment of the title "architect" (as opposed to "housewright" or "builder") by Benjamin Latrobe and others at the beginning of the nineteenth century, highlights of the evolution include the first professional organization of architects in New York in 1836 (the American Institution of Architects), the formation of the American Institute of Architects in 1857, the appearance of architectural periodicals in the 1860s and 1870s, and the establishment of university-level architectural instruction at MIT in 1868. By the 1880s architecture, driven by technological developments, industrialism, and the growth of cities, had become a complex and sophisticated profession. Daniel

Burnham summarized the situation eloquently in this speech to the Illinois A.I.A. in 1890, which is quoted at length here because it is apropos and because Wright must surely have heard it or read it:

An architect used to find little difficulty in designing pretty much everything needed by the people, from a court house to a cottage. He made some sketches which he called working drawings, and some notes which went under the name of specifications. There was not much competition in the trades. Bosses were capable mechanics and honest men, and would carry out the work intrusted to them with fidelity, no matter what the price. To lay out a plan and construct a building were the principal duties of an architect.

Now, however, he is confronted with much more serious problems. Public taste has become trained and critical, and is constantly becoming more so. The designer must now be very talented and thoroughly trained to obtain any permanent recognition.

Business buildings are doubled and tripled in height, and are fireproof, where they were mostly low and combustible ten years ago. The constructor, therefore, must be a great engineer, wise, wary, and of soundest judgment; for not only must he build safely, but not a pound of steel or a cubic foot of concrete or a brick too much can be tolerated. He must not only guarantee stability, but must produce it without the unnecessary waste of a single dollar. Economy is demanded by our keen, intelligent building public almost more rigorously than good plans or good art.

Buildings are now supplied with complex heating, plumbing, sewerage, ventilation, elevators, pumps, tanks, engines, dynamos and electric lighting. Many have costly plants of all these kinds, none are without a part. The owners have a right to expect the very best of everything in every part, and perfect mechanical planning and application in each case. Therefore very expert mechanical and sanitary engineering are required to handle this part of the work.

If many important works be on hand in an office at once, the mere handling of the business they produce requires much experience, and is enough to occupy the time of an able man.

Passing over many other strong points that might be instanced, I have shown enough to prove that one man cannot himself attend to all the work of a modern city practice in America, and as we agree that "attention to details" is necessary to success, it is plain that some method must be found to attain it, other than through a mixed practice by a single person *in the old way*.

It is manifest that the successful practitioner of the future will be a specialist, or at the head of an organization of specialists. This is not an original statement on my part. It was made to the Illinois State Association of Architects some years ago in a letter written by Mr. Richard T. Crane, of Chicago, in response to a circular sent out by the association to prominent business men, asking for criticism on the then usual conduct of an architect's office.

To design and construct a great office building, some stores and flats, some dwellings, some factories, a church, etc., in a manner to elicit praise from our critical building public, is beyond the powers of one man's brain and energy, if he attend to the details of all. If, therefore, a man or a firm is ambitious to carry on a great general practice, there must be in the organization:

A very great designer.
An exceptionally strong chief engineer.
A sanitary engineer.
A mechanical engineer.
A business man.

Each of these will have his hands full if he is faithful, and only with such an organization, I say again, can a large general practice live and keep going.[31]

Burnham's point was familiar to Wright from his experiences with Adler and Sullivan. Over the course of nearly six years there, he was given increasingly large responsibilities: he designed the firm's office plan in the Auditorium tower; he was given any domestic commissions that came to the firm; he was made chief of the office's thirty draftsmen; and he apparently had a major role in some of the firm's best-known works, such as the Schiller Building.[32] If he had intended eventually to establish a similar practice for himself, he would have noted that Adler and Sullivan, like Burnham and Root, Holabird and Roche, Jenney and Mundie, and other large "general practice" firms, divided design, engineering, and business among two or more principal partners.

Wright was also familiar with the operations of smaller domestic design offices such as those of Joseph Lyman Silsbee, where he spent most of 1887; Beers, Clay and Dutton, where he worked briefly; and his friend Cecil Corwin, with whom he shared an office in the Schiller Building in 1893. Of Silsbee's office Wright wrote: "The office system was bad. Silsbee got a ground plan and made his pretty sketch, getting some charming picturesque effect he had in his mind. Then the sketch would come out into the draughting room to be fixed up into a building, keeping the floor-plan near the sketch if possible."[33]

It seems that the formation of Wright's approach to practice, like his design for the Prairie House, did not crystallize suddenly when he left Sullivan's office in 1893. The decision to design at home in Oak Park and maintain an office in Chicago appears to have begun as a compromise between a desire to maintain contact with colleagues and clients in the city and the pull of opposing forces that were intensifying as Wright's practice matured during the 1890s. Among these forces nature, the touchstone of all of Wright's architectural thinking, must have been especially powerful: many of his photographs from the 1890s are of trees, shrubs, flowers, and weeds found around his home or in nearby fields and meadows.

Wright's ultimate choice of living and working in one environment, close to his family and to nature, not only is wholly consistent with the organicism of his mature architectural principles but traces back to his boyhood experiences on the Lloyd-Jones farm in Spring Green, Wisconsin (a similarly self-contained, organic environment), and forward to the institutionalization of that way of life in the Taliesin Fellowship. It is no wonder, in the light of his principles and preferences, that he grew increasingly hostile toward the city environment as he matured.

Yet the city was a logical place for someone who intended to pursue architecture on the scale of Adler and Sullivan or Burnham and Root. Can one conclude that Wright's decision to locate his practice in Oak Park was tied to a decision to specialize in domestic architecture? Daniel Burnham had recommended specialized over general practice in his 1890 speech to the A.I.A.:

> But why "look" for a general practice when all conditions about us prove that specialists do better work, and in the long run get the greatest rewards. . . . Let one or more take up dwellings, others churches, others hotels, others business buildings. Let each aim to make the public say from San Francisco to New York, "He is the master in that line, if you want the best, you *must* go to him"; and then, I ask, will there be any doubt about a great name for you, or a great fortune?[34]

There is ample evidence that Wright was well on his way to being identified as a domestic specialist even before he left Adler and Sullivan, and Robert Twombly argues persuasively that he was drawn to domestic architecture by deep-seated psychological forces.[35] Moreover, he would surely have observed that in 1893, thanks to the efforts of the Chicago School, tall-building design was far in advance of domestic design, where historicism continued to reign. The opportunity was clearly there.

Despite these considerations, and an obvious preoccupation with domestic design that continued throughout his career, it is unlikely that Wright deliberately sought domestic specialization and that the Oak Park studio was conceived to further such a goal. He possessed a powerful will to design that transcended boundaries and categories. He designed everything from books and dresses to gasoline stations. He designed large commercial buildings whenever he could; if he mostly obtained commissions for houses, it was because others identified him with domestic architecture. Early in his career the Oak Park studio functioned as a kind of laboratory where he had the space and the freedom to work out on a small scale some of the fundamental design concepts—the pinwheel plan of his house; the bi-nuclear arrangement of the studio and library; the two-story space and interlocking geometries of the studio—that would reappear in larger forms in commissions throughout his career.

The creation of the home and studio complex was also significant because it enabled Wright to shift the nature of his office organization decisively away from the atmosphere of regimentation and hostility toward draftsmen that he had witnessed in the Adler and Sullivan office [36] and toward a master-apprentice relationship that was more personal, informal, and even familial. Grant Manson described this arrangement in Beaux-Arts terms. [37] James O'Gorman more plausibly describes its likely model as H. H. Richardson's home-studio in Brookline, Massachusetts, which was available to Wright through Marianna Griswold Van Rensselaer's description in her 1888 monograph on Richardson. [38] But a model much closer to Wright's sphere of interest at that time than either the Beaux-Arts or Richardson was the Arts and Crafts movement.

The Arts and Crafts movement began in England as a reaction against the social ills and dehumanized factory-made goods of the industrial revolution. Inspired by the writings of Thomas Carlyle, A. W. N. Pugin, and especially John Ruskin, and led by William Morris, small groups of artists and craftsmen began forming during the 1870s and 1880s in an effort to recapture the moral values, social structures, and artistic traditions of the medieval world. The Century Guild was formed by Arthur MacMurdo in 1882, the Art Workers Guild in 1884, and the School and Guild of Handicraft and the Arts and Crafts Exhibition Society in 1888.

Through the medium of books, periodicals, goods, and word of mouth the Arts and Crafts movement soon gained a foothold in North America, and Chicago became an active center. It is difficult to pinpoint when this happened (though the formation of the Chicago Arts and Crafts Society in 1897 is certainly significant), and even more difficult to determine how and when Frank Lloyd Wright became conscious of the movement. By the time of his "Art and Craft of the Machine" address at Hull House in 1901, a critique of Ruskin's and Morris's ideas probably formulated during the 1890s, the Arts and Crafts movement had been in the air in Chicago for at least a decade. According to David Hanks, William Morris products were available at the Marshall Field Store as early as the 1880s. Jane Addams and Ellen Gates Starr had visited Toynbee Hall in London, a model for Hull House, the first American settlement house, in 1888. Walter Crane, a distinguished English book illustrator with strong connections to the Arts and Crafts movement there, exhibited and lectured at the Chicago Art Institute in 1892, and Joseph Twymon, another English exponent of the movement, settled in Chicago and promoted the ideas of Ruskin and Morris. [39]

Hull House became the focus of the Chicago movement, and it was there that the Chicago Arts and Crafts Society was founded, with Wright as a charter member, in 1897. [40] In 1902

Wright wrote to the English craftsman-architect C. R. Ashbee, whom he had met in Chicago in 1900, "I caught at your name in the 'Review' [presumably the *Architectural Review,* London] some time ago and read your article in one of our magazines. You see my ears are pricked up for news of you and my eyes are on the watch for signs of your work."[41] These contacts, and the likelihood that Wright kept abreast of the English periodicals, suggest that he had ample opportunity to know of the guildlike communal life-style of Morris and his followers. It is not suggested that this life-style supplied a specific model for the working arrangement of Wright's home and studio in Oak Park. Rather, it was simply inherent in the philosophy of the Arts and Crafts movement that art activity should take place in a spirit of brotherhood, mutual respect, and familial intimacy rather than in the brusque, tense world of nineteenth-century big business.

CONCLUSION

According to his autobiography, Wright established his own architectural practice in 1893 as a result of his disagreement with Louis Sullivan over the "bootlegged" houses, but surely, after five and a half years at the heart of the Chicago School, he was *ready* to be independent. The World's Columbian Exposition of 1893 may have provided impetus for that decision.

Following the tradition established by the first such fair, the Great Exhibition of 1851 in London, the Chicago Fair was principally dedicated to the display of new technologies. Entire large buildings were given over to electricity, mining, transportation, and machinery, and the largest, George Post's 1,687-foot-long, 312-foot-high Manufactures Building, was charac-

terized in the literature of the Fair as "the largest building ever built by man" and as the "central object of the Fair."[42] Whatever speculation has been forced upon us by Wright's reticence concerning his life in Chicago between 1887 and 1893, his employment on Adler and Sullivan's Transportation Building placed him squarely in the middle of this grand gathering of nineteenth-century technology. For a few months in 1893 the world was at Wright's fingertips—not to have, but to understand and to assess.

Something was amiss in this world, however. There was a discrepancy between the purely functional nature of the Fair's technological exhibitions and the classicizing of the buildings that housed them. Louis Sullivan registered his objections to the Beaux-Arts theme of the Fair in his nonclassical design for the Transportation Building and in his statement, published much later, that "the damage wrought by the World's Fair will last for half a century from its date, if not longer."[43] That Wright shared Sullivan's disdain for the Fair's classicism became apparent less than a year later when he rejected Daniel Burnham's offer of six expense-free years at the Ecole des Beaux-Arts and in Rome on the grounds that "he [Sullivan] has helped spoil the Beaux Arts for me."[44] Sullivan, however, remained indifferent to the full implications of the machine for architecture, a problem that continued to preoccupy Wright through the 1890s and led to his essay "The Art and Craft of the Machine" and the first Prairie houses of 1901.

One other discrepancy in the Fair's architecture may have come to Wright's attention. Within a ten-minute walk from Adler and Sullivan's Transportation Building, on the Midway Plaisance, one could encounter an impressive array of world architecture in reproduction: representative buildings from most European countries, many from Latin America, and others from the Far East. An entire street from Cairo was re-created, and the periphery of the Midway was sprinkled with villages of Javanese, Bedouins, Samoans, Laplanders, and Native Americans inhabited by indigenous peoples in their native costumes and with their furnishings, livestock, and trappings. For Wright the Midway Plaisance might be considered an equivalent to the architectural history class that students take today, if not richer in its palpability and its global breadth.

In the buildings of the Midway Plaisance it is possible to identify influences on Wright's subsequent work. In the Japanese Ho-o-den Grant Manson recognized sources for the Prairie House.[45] In the octagonal core and layered roof of the Ceylonese Building one finds echoes of Wright's River Forest Tennis Club of 1906. In the sumptuous gathering of furniture, carpets, and other decorative arts in the East India Building and the Ceylonese Tea Room it is possible to recognize the inspiration for Wright's early collections in his Oak Park home. And the fragments from Uxmal constitute Wright's earliest known contact with the Mayan inspiration for his A. D. German Warehouse of 1915 and his California textile block houses of the 1920s.

It may be, however, that Wright drew a more comprehensive lesson from the stylistic discrepancies of the Fair. The unmistakable distinctiveness of national character expressed in the buildings of Ceylon, Norway, China, Spain, and many other countries had no counterpart among the derivative American exhibition buildings. America led the world in industrial technology but lacked an architecture of its own. We cannot be certain that Wright saw the Fair this way, but his subsequent achievement in creating a distinctive American architecture suggests that the Fair not only gave him much to think about, but helped persuade him that it was time to get on with his career.

## NOTES

I would like to thank Donald Hoffmann for reading this manuscript and for making numerous valuable suggestions regarding its content.

1. Frank Lloyd Wright, *An Autobiography* (New York, 1943), p. 110.

2. Vincent Scully, *The Shingle Style and the Stick Style* (New Haven, 1955), pp. 155–164; see also Scully's "American Houses: Thomas Jefferson to Frank Lloyd Wright," in Edgar Kaufmann, Jr., ed., *The Rise of an American Architecture* (New York, 1970), pp. 163–209.

3. The best account of Wright's personal life is Robert Twombly's *Frank Lloyd Wright: An Interpretive Biography* (New York, 1973).

4. Carl Condit, *The Chicago School* (Chicago, 1974); Sigfried Giedion, *Space, Time and Architecture* (Cambridge, Mass., 1971); William Jordy, *American Buildings and Their Architects: Progressive and Academic Ideals at the Turn of the Twentieth Century* (New York, 1976).

5. Wright, *An Autobiography*, pp. 89–111.

6. Frank Lloyd Wright, "The Art and Craft of the Machine," in Edgar Kaufmann and Ben Raeburn, eds., *Frank Lloyd Wright: Writings and Buildings* (New York, 1960), pp. 55–73.

7. Bruce Brooks Pfeiffer, ed., *Treasures of Taliesin: Seventy-Six Unbuilt Designs of Frank Lloyd Wright* (Fresno, Calif.; Carbondale, Ill., 1985), Plates 36a, 36b, and 36c and accompanying text.

8. Illustrated in W. Jordy, *American Buildings*, Fig. 140.

9. Dankmar Adler, "The Chicago Auditorium," *Architectural Record*, 1 (April–June 1892), pp. 425–434.

10. "Ventilating and Heating the Chicago National Bank," *Engineering Record*, 44 (November 23, 1901), pp. 502–504.

11. Margaret Ingels, *Willis Carrier, Father of Air-Conditioning* (Garden City, N.Y., 1952), p. 17.

12. Letter from Darwin Martin to John Larkin, March 20, 1903, Mss, Darwin Martin Papers, Archives of the State University of New York at Buffalo.

13. "Larkin Company Administration Building Frank Lloyd Wright Architect 1903 Specifications," Archives of the Frank Lloyd Wright Memorial Foundation.

14. Wright, *An Autobiography*, p. 80.

15. Frank Lloyd Wright, *Genius and the Mobocracy* (New York, 1971), p. 70.

16. James F. O'Gorman, "Henry Hobson Richardson and Frank Lloyd Wright," *Art Quarterly,* 32 (August 1969), pp. 292–315.

17. Wright, *An Autobiography,* p. 103; *Genius and the Mobocracy,* pp. 70 and 76.

18. Wright, *An Autobiography,* p. 103; *Genius and the Mobocracy,* p. 72.

19. Wright, *Genius and the Mobocracy,* p. 63.

20. Wright, *An Autobiography,* p. 270.

21. *Ibid.,* p. 103.

22. Wright, *Genius and the Mobocracy,* p. 55.

23. Wright, *An Autobiography,* p. 107.

24. Wright, *Genius and the Mobocracy,* p. 74.

25. *Ibid.,* p. 77.

26. Grant C. Manson, *Frank Lloyd Wright to 1910: The First Golden Age* (New York, 1958), p. 215.

27. *Ibid.,* p. 44.

28. *Ibid.,* p. 46.

29. *Ibid.*

30. *Ibid.,* p. 44.

31. Daniel Burnham, "Association Notes," *Inland Architect and News Record,* 15 (June 1890), p. 76.

32. According to Wright's account in *An Autobiography,* pp. 107, 110, and 123; and in *Genius and the Mobocracy,* p. 62.

33. Wright, *An Autobiography,* pp. 70–71.

34. Burnham, "Association Notes," *Inland Architect,* p. 76.

35. Twombly, *Frank Lloyd Wright,* pp. 26–50.

36. Wright, *Genius and the Mobocracy,* p. 70.

37. Manson, *Frank Lloyd Wright to 1910,* p. 46.

38. O'Gorman, "Henry Hobson Richardson and Frank Lloyd Wright," *Art Quarterly,* 32 (August 1969), p. 311.

39. David A. Hanks, "Chicago and the Midwest," in Robert Judson Clark, ed., *The Arts and Crafts Movement in America, 1876–1916* (Princeton, 1972), p. 58.

40. Gwendolyn Wright, *Moralism and the Model Home* (Chicago, 1980), p. 128.

41. Frank Lloyd Wright to C. R. Ashbee, January 3, 1902, reprinted in Alan Crawford, "Ten Letters from Frank Lloyd Wright to Charles Robert Ashbee," *Architectural History,* 13 (1970), p. 65.

42. *The Dream City: A Portfolio of Photographic Views of the World's Columbian Exposition* (St. Louis, 1893), unpaged.

43. Louis H. Sullivan, *The Autobiography of an Idea* (New York, 1956), p. 325.

44. Wright, *An Autobiography,* p. 126.

45. Manson, *Frank Lloyd Wright to 1910,* pp. 34–40.

# ORGANIC ARCHITECTURE: THE PRINCIPLES OF FRANK LLOYD WRIGHT

*Aaron G. Green, F.A.I.A.*

It is over forty years since I first encountered Frank Lloyd Wright's concept of organic architecture. It changed my life.

Surely in time it must similarly have inspired many men and women throughout the world. Mies van der Rohe has described the effect of Wright's seminal work at the beginning of this century:

This, then, was the situation in 1910.

At this moment, so critical for us, there came to Berlin the exhibition of the work of Frank Lloyd Wright. This comprehensive display and the extensive publication of his works enabled us really to become acquainted with the achievement of this architect. The encounter was destined to prove of greatest significance to the development of architecture in Europe.

The work of this great master revealed an architectural world of unexpected force and clarity of language, and also a disconcerting richness of form. Here, finally, was a master-builder drawing upon the veritable fountain-head of architecture, who with true originality lifted his architectural creations into the light. Here, again, at last, genuine organic architecture flowered.

Aaron G. Green studied at Alabama State College, the Chicago Academy of Fine Arts, and Cooper Union for the Advancement of Science and Art, in New York City. He was a Taliesin Fellow from 1939 to 1942. He established his architectural practice in San Francisco in 1951, and represented Frank Lloyd Wright on the West Coast until 1959. He was a Visiting Lecturer at Stanford University from 1957 to 1972. He has received a number of prestigious architectural awards.

. . . The dynamic impulse emanating from his work invigorated a whole generation. His influence was strongly felt even when it was not actually visible.

. . . In his undiminishing power he resembles a giant tree in a wide landscape, which, year after year, ever attains a more noble crown.[1]

Those, however, who are offended by an unorthodox idea or by innovation, or are resentful of change in custom, are inevitably the most voluble; and from the beginning their reaction against the mere mention of organic architecture was violent and widespread, particularly among critics, experts, and academics.

My own experience with organic architecture has been a profoundly positive one. For twenty years I had the privilege of a close association with Frank Lloyd Wright, both personal and professional. I began as an apprentice, and during the last eight years of his life was his architectural associate and his West Coast representative, working out of the joint office he requested that we open together in San Francisco in 1951. During that eventful relationship I grew to understand that his integrity as a person and his practice of organic architecture were inextricable. The conduct of his life in its daily details was one and the same with his work as an architect and his devotion to the understanding of nature.

He was constantly moved to demonstrate that the principles

of organic architecture were not alone a method of building but contained the elements of a more creative and fuller way of life. In his book *A Testament* (1957) he wrote: "All buildings built should serve the liberation of mankind, liberating the lives of individuals. What amazing beauty would be ours if man's spirit, thus organic, should learn to characterize this new free life of ours in America as natural." The very fundamentals that he could demonstrate more directly in buildings than in words were the core of the lectures and writings in which he clarified his views on politics, economics, business, land planning, farming, education, and whatever other disciplines, personal or public, claimed his attention.

For the true meaning of Wright's term "organic architecture" one must look beyond a simple definition, or a collection of axioms, or a formula for the design of buildings. To begin with, *organic* can be seen as a convenient one-word reference to the complex synthesis of principles that were most clearly expressed in his earliest writings and evident in his earliest architectural works. The term as used in those early years never changed in meaning. For the sake of simplicity one might substitute for *organic* the word *natural*, often used by Wright in conjunction with *logic* ("natural logic," "nature's logic") or the word *rational*, which he also often used; but he much preferred *organic*.

For all the efforts of academicians, historians, architectural critics, and others to analyze Wright's work, his own voluminous writings offer the clearest and most direct guide to his thinking. His intent was always educational. His fundamental concerns were with human dignity, with individual freedom and democracy, with human endeavor on its highest altruistic plane, and with enriching the relationship of the individual to his or her environment. His inner strength and convictions were intensified and matured by constant reference to those he regarded as great creative minds, among them Victor Hugo, William Blake, William Morris, Laotze, Viollet-le-Duc, Jefferson, Emerson, Thoreau, Louis Sullivan, and Dankmar Adler.

The synthesis of the fundamentals inherent in a more meaningful life was so simple and instinctive in his thinking that he had difficulty at times in perceiving the inadequacy of the term *organic* to convey this synthesis to others. Architecture he saw as the Master Art. Also necessary for a full life were music, poetry, and above all nature—the white clouds against the blue sky, the shimmering dew on the morning's grasses, the structural silhouetted form of the oak tree in winter—all freely available to all people, all necessary for life-giving enjoyment. In time, couldn't everyone see this, understand it, and live it? That hope moved him to write, to exhort, to criticize, and to demonstrate a more fulfilling way.

Often quoting William Blake's "exuberance is beauty," Wright stressed the joy of understanding nature by observation—nature, which produces the forms of plants, each responsive to the needs of its environment, each with its basic "engineering" structure, its material and color, its form and function evolving in its life's pattern. Carrying the concept "form follows function" a conclusive step further into "form and function are one," Wright threw new light on a major tenet of organic architecture. The building must have its own form, its beauty emergent from its consonance with nature.

As we pass along the wayside some blossom with unusually glowing color or prettiness of form attracts us. Held by it we gratefully accept its perfect loveliness. But, seeking the secret of its ineffable charm, we find the blossom whose more obvious claim first arrested our attention as nature intended, intimately related to the texture and shape of the foliage beneath it. We discover peculiar sympathy between the form of this flower and the system upon which leaves are arranged about the stalk. From this we are led on to observe a characteristic habit of growth and discover a resultant pattern of structure having first direction toward form deep down in roots hidden in the warm earth, kept moist there by a conservative covering of leaf-mould. Structure—as now we may observe—proceeds from generals to particulars arriving at the blossom, to attract us, proclaiming in its lines and form the Nature of the structure that bore it. We have here a thing organic. Law and order are the basis of a finished grace and beauty. "Beauty" is the expression of fundamental conditions in line, form and color true to those conditions and seeming to exist to fulfill them according to some thoughtful original design.[2]

Wright's philosophy of organic architecture is not to be confused with his singular style. That style is unique, his personal form of expression. He often repeated his hope that other architects and students would not imitate him but develop their own individuality. The principles of organic architecture, he believed, were not related to any particular style but were adaptable to all architectural solutions: "Given similar conditions, similar tools, similar people, similar language, I believe architects will, with proper regard for the organic nature of the thing produced arrive at greatly varied results; buildings sufficiently harmonious with each other and more and more so with great individuality."[3]

However many of Wright's building plans and forms we consider, we can always recognize the principles at work. The degree of the relationship of a building to its site and environment determines the degree of its harmony, the aim being always, as Wright said, "to make the landscape more beautiful than before that building was built."

A superb example is the Marin County Civic Center in San Rafael, California. When he first visited the site, after a twenty-minute review of the hilly terrain in a jeep, Wright turned to me and, making wave-like motions with his hand, declared, "I know what to do here. We will bridge these hills with graceful arches." My voluminous administrative and space-requirement analysis for the project emphasized the need for flexibility to accommodate internal departmental changes. Wright quickly assimilated that information, designed the project, and indicated the forms of the various functional building components requested. Three months later, when I was asked to come to Taliesin to "see what we have done," I was proudly shown the first sketches, which conformed precisely to his initial inspiration for the design. All broad functional aspects of exterior traffic circulation and the relationship of building to topography were beautifully resolved; so also were the basic structural concepts. For interior function Wright had designed a continuous space of two different widths, a space free of column interference and filled with light and air from its internal atrium "mall" and its exterior protected balcony fenestration. Such space would obviously allow the required flexibility for relocating interior partitions, all nonstructural. On that occasion at Taliesin, Wright said to me: "Now you can do whatever you want with the inside; it's completely flexible, as you wished." In a speech to the citizens of Marin County prior to construction of the project, he stated, "Here is a crucial opportunity to open the eyes of the entire country to what officials gathering together might themselves do to broaden and beautify human lives." Today from the interior of the building each of the graceful arches, large or small, inevitably frames a view, repeating that earlier wave motion of his hand and circumscribing the form of one of the surrounding hills.

Subsequently, a system was developed that allowed partitions, lights, electrical outlets, and so forth, to be located at any place on a grid 32 inches square, a remarkably flexible arrangement that has been utilized with great success for many years and is a continuing tribute to his original organic design concept. All state-of-the-art technology had been designed into the scheme to create beauty, economy, and rational functional relationships. This skylighted mall concept and form has since directly influenced many copies throughout the contemporary architectural scene.

Contrary to a general misconception, Frank Lloyd Wright was not dictatorial in considering the needs of his clients, nor was he adamant against changes. I have been present on various occasions when he agreed to a client's request for a functional revision, seemingly relishing the opportunity to improve the design. Only if a request appeared frivolous or illogical, or violated his aesthetic principles, would he be steadfast in opposition.

Again and again his creative virtuosity allowed him to resolve all basic functional requirements in his initial concept for the form of a building. Since the plan developed first, the functional concept was the established priority. When I submitted a "bubble diagram" to him to illustrate a client's desired functional relationships for a commercial project, the Degnan-Donohoe Restaurant project for Yosemite National Park, Wright, probably having predetermined a circular scheme, used my diagram directly as the basis for the plan of the building.

Such projects as the Larkin Building in Buffalo in 1904 early demonstrated his mastery of functional programs for use by industry and commerce. Later many others were to come, among them the Monona Terrace project for Madison, Wisconsin; the Rogers Lacy Hotel project for Dallas; the Johnson Administration Building and Research Tower in Racine, Wis-

consin; Florida Southern College in Lakeland; the Kalita Humphreys Theatre in Dallas; and the Marin County Civic Center. One of his last commissions was a lyrically beautiful and workable solution for the administration and production of electronic components and systems for the Lenkurt Electric Company Building in San Carlos, California, a project with which I was also associated. Unfortunately the building was not built because the company was sold to a less perceptive owner just as construction was about to begin.

Many of Wright's innovations provided a new direction for freedom and logic in architectural design, and all emphasized the importance of an overall sense of unity and harmony. The sense-of-shelter within the continuous vista of his building—sculptured, as it was, into differentiated functional areas—provided a wholly new experience, visual and sensual, spiritual and emotional, with fresh elements of space, color, and form continuing to surprise and delight.

Wright enjoyed exploring all the characteristics of whatever material he chose to use. In most cases his buildings were predominantly of one basic material or a combination of two primary ones. Most of the early houses were stone or brick masonry in combination with plaster, plus wood as accent material. The Usonian houses were primarily of wood with some masonry. Later there was the unique reinforced concrete and stone masonry combination of "Fallingwater," the house for Edgar Kaufmann in Mill Run, Pennsylvania; and the use of reinforced concrete block, usually pattern-textured, earthquake-resistant for California. Several public structures emphasized brick (the Johnson Administration Building) and precast and/or poured concrete (Unity Temple in Oak Park, Illinois; the Guggenheim Museum in New York; the Greek Orthodox

Church in Wauwatosa, Wisconsin; the Marin County Civic Center; the Monona Terrace project). In all cases the form was integral with the material. Of his early insight into the nature of materials, Wright wrote: "I began to learn to see brick as brick, I learned to see wood as wood and learned to see concrete or glass or metal each for itself and all as themselves."[4]

The "unit system" was a very important part of the organic process of design and construction. Just as the warp is discipline for a woven textile, and as the scale and notes are disciplines for the composer of music, so Wright used the unit system as a discipline for design. The choice of unit system was in harmony with the nature and pattern of the construction, and with the spirit and "grammar" of the design. Later in his career he felt much more free to explore unit systems of circles, hexagons, triangles—occasionally in combination—as well as the square and rectangular units of earlier years.

The unit system not only provided a tool for design, but also unified and simplified the construction process as it developed a modular system for the fabrication of parts, by means of a repetition of sizes of components such as windows and doors, with related dimensions throughout. In practice, the workmen, once they became familiar with the process, were grateful. Since carpentry and masonry tools were designed for 90-degree and 45-degree angles, the workmen had to adjust at first to the 120-degree-angle hexagons and 60-degree-angle equilateral triangles used in many Usonian houses of the later period. However, once they created templates to serve as layout tools for these angles, it became a simplified construction discipline, with all parts related in a direct geometry.

Invariably after completing construction of a Wright build-ing its workmen were awed and proud of what they had produced. Their enthusiasm often bolstered the owner's morale after his experience of the delays and difficulties inherent in varying from a standard building process.

The term "grammar of the building" was frequently used by Wright to indicate the individual characteristics that make a building what it is. Just as the flora and fauna of the sea or the desert develop individual characteristics of color, form, and structure relating directly to their environment, function, and nature—their "grammar"—so also does Frank Lloyd Wright's organic building develop its individual thematic correctness, proper to its environment, while incorporating the special functional needs and/or idiosyncrasies of its user.

Although Wright always emphasized the priority of the plan, in his work the plan and the building forms were inspired simultaneously by his amazing ability to synthesize all factors of environment and need. When he sat down at the drafting table, he had already visualized the project design in its overall aspects. Always the floor plan or plot plan was developed first; it was on the topographical map of the property that he worked, with all site factors known and generally indicated. He had also absorbed, prior to developing his design sketch, the client's program of needs and desires. Amazingly the full form of the building emerged from his pencil as a flower unfolding, without hesitancy and as a continuous drawing operation from plan to elevation to cross-sections, with some notes and dimensions to denote important aspects; and always drawn in direct relationship to the particular unit system he had chosen as appropriate. Once when I remarked on how easily and quickly he had developed a solution for a complex project design, he replied, "Yes, but you must realize how much time I spend [mentally] designing before I sit down to draw."

In the next stage, a designated staff member would transfer Wright's original sketch into a more precise line drawing. The original sketch was invariably correct and workable in its engineering, its relationship of functional and structural parts, and its relationship to site. During this stage Wright was always close by to monitor further development of the drawings at the staff member's board, to elaborate with more technical details, and to answer the draftsman's technical design questions—and always with spontaneity and the greatest of ease.

Wright's legacy to society includes many things that have become so much part of our daily life that their origins in his innovation are forgotten. Some of them: indirect lighting, ribbon and corner windows, plate glass commercial entrance doors, steel office furniture, and even the wall-hung toilet used in most commercial buildings.

Always concerned with new technical developments, Wright was quick to incorporate into his creative thinking those he found of particular interest. He also often explored design ideas to improve manufactured objects in daily use. He was fascinated by fine motorcars; and though he often criticized the normal output of Detroit, one of the automobiles he particularly enjoyed was the first model of the Lincoln Continental (1939), a long, sleek convertible, and the following year's Lincoln, a sedan. (He improved its lines by a partial modification, a custom design for the top.) He always had his cars painted a rusty red color affectionately called "Taliesin Red." For him red was the color of life, the most "organic" color. It could be seen on many objects at Taliesin.

In 1957 while on a visit to Taliesin West in Arizona about a project I was associated with, I was asked early one morning to come to Mr. Wright's bedroom. Still in pajamas, he was working at a drawing board near his bed. Saying that his insomnia had generated a desire to get some ideas down on paper during the night, he proudly showed me rough sketches of his designs for a three-wheeled automobile and a vertical-takeoff aircraft. Knowing that I had experience as a pilot, he called me in at such an early hour because he wanted to discuss physics related to the flying machine. I was able to explain the aerodynamic principles of "uplift" as it related to the cross-sectional design of the typical aircraft wing. I recall that very privileged experience whenever I see the published designs for the vehicles accompanying his Broadacre City dissertation in his book *The Living City*. It was all a part of organic architecture.

Another example of organic design in areas not normally invaded by architects was the "Butterfly Wing" bridge in 1949 for a second crossing of San Francisco Bay. The location was under consideration by the State Bridge Authority, and a local structural engineer who wished to participate with calculations for the design asked Wright to develop a design proposal. The concept utilized a variety of advanced engineering and construction techniques such as precast and prestressed lightweight concrete and chemical soil solidification. It was of thin-shell monocoque form with a cantilevered roadway, using a ribbed cross-section design resembling that of an airplane wing for most of the low-level crossing. At the shipping channel the crossing made a transition to a great arch spanning the required height and width. The arch provided a split roadway, enclosing, in its center, a small park with a fine view of the city skyline. For concrete the structure would be remarkably light in weight. Its basic construction concept included on-shore precasting of major sections, which would then be barged to the installation point.

The design received little notice. Later, when I showed Wright a picture of the proposed steel "Erector-set" design for the Richmond–San Rafael Bridge (since constructed), he agreed to cooperate with efforts I suggested to publicize his bridge design. "In view of the horrible thing they are about to construct," he said, "it will be in the name of much needed education."

A model of the bridge was constructed, poised on a mirror-covered table 16 feet in diameter, and was displayed at San Francisco museums and other prominent locations. The media and citizens in general appeared excited by the proposal, but as usual with most of Wright's innovative projects, the engineering fraternity said either "It can't be done" or "It will cost too much." Governor Goodwin Knight felt obligated to request a presentation, which Wright and I jointly made to the Governor and a large group of his department heads at a lunch meeting. Few questions were asked; obviously the interest was only token. On the flight back to San Francisco, Wright remarked, "We can't expect politicians and engineers to understand." Yet the San Francisco Bay area did enjoy some residual benefits: the two subsequent bridges constructed as South Bay crossings are low-level reinforced concrete bridges, albeit not as advanced in design or construction techniques.

One of Wright's unflagging hopes was to solve the housing problem for people with limited budgets. He liked particularly prospective clients who came to him with limited funds but with such a perceptive appreciation of the master architect's work that they were ready to construct a Wright build-ing with their own hands if necessary. That kind of person always obtained a design, and several of Wright's residential projects were built in that way.

One in which I participated was a dramatic example of Wright's organic designing: The construction was to be of rammed earth (*pisé de terre*), a method used in many parts of the world dating back to prehistoric times. I was pleased to be the catalyst for the Cooperative Homesteads project and its concept materials. The project was designed in the early 1940s for a site near Detroit. Twenty families had banded together to build their own housing units on a 160-acre farm parcel. They also expected to raise crops on this land as a source of income during periods of unemployment in the auto industry.

After assisting Wright in producing drawings and acting as liaison with the group, I spent several months setting up the project and getting the first prototypical building started. Wartime legislation made it necessary for us to obtain "defense housing" status in order to purchase equipment such as secondhand earth-handling and pneumatic-ramming equipment, and to experiment with bitulithic additives and new techniques for expediting the labor-intensive earth construction. The labor demands of the war effort reduced the work force considerably, but we managed to accomplish enough construction to validate the techniques. When the Army Air Corps snatched me away for training, the project drainage system was still under construction. Without a construction superintendent and without the anticipated workers, with the drainage system incomplete, the project became a fatality of the war, literally washed away.

Another self-help project fared better but had a tragic end.

In 1950 Robert Berger asked Wright to design a house for San Anselmo, California, which he would build completely himself (with very limited funds), the fee to be paid on the installment plan. Berger, good with his hands and his mind, dedicated his efforts and his family's to a fine job of construction, perfect in every detail. (Wright's smallest commission was doubtless the design for a dog house requested by Berger's young son and built concurrently with the house.) Building the house was a continuous task of love for fifteen years, performed in addition to Berger's job as a teacher; during much of that time he and his family occupied the house in unfinished condition. And then, with only a few small details left to complete, Bob Berger unexpectedly died. At Wright's request I had assisted him with professional advice and interpretation of plans gratis for the full period.

Probably the most successful of the Frank Lloyd Wright designs executed entirely by owners was that for Mr. and Mrs. Don Lovness in Stillwater, Minnesota. Two dwellings—a main house and a guesthouse—were both exquisitely constructed, together with all furniture, light fixtures, and other accoutrements as designed by Wright. Virginia Lovness, a gifted artist, personally accomplished a great deal of the construction while her chemist husband was at work. The Lovnesses' family life developed around the construction of their houses and was a true assimilation of Wright's principle of organic architecture as a way of life. Indeed, most clients of his that I have met freely state that the experience of organic architecture, whether or not they had personal contact with the architect himself, has been the most important influence in their lives.

Wright's interest in every detail of building knew no boundaries. After the basic grammar of form and structure must come the detailed items for use and delight, carrying out the same theme with color, texture, contrasts of dark and light, and changes of scale. This involved loving concern for design and harmonious relationships of all furniture, lighting, carpets, textiles, "stained" glass, sculptured or other integral ornamentation, and at times such accessories as china, silverware, and flower vases. In his earlier years little could be obtained in the marketplace to harmonize with his buildings—residential, commercial, or public—and much had to be made by skilled craftsmen to specific orders. In the later years, thanks in part to his growing influence, more acceptable furniture, textiles, hardware, lamps, and so forth began to be available, and this gave him much pleasure. Indeed he had predicted it:

> In Organic Architecture then, it is quite impossible to consider the building as one thing, its furnishings another and setting and environment still another. The Spirit in which these buildings are conceived sees all these together as one thing. . . . The very chairs and tables, cabinets and even musical instruments, where practicable, are of the building itself, never fixtures upon it.
>
> . . . To make these necessary appurtenances elements, themselves sufficiently light, graceful and flexible features of the informal use of an abode, requires much more time and thought on my part as well as more money to spend than is usually forthcoming in our country at this time. But in time this will be accomplished by improvements in all stock articles.[5]

Fortunately, only a few of his clients, or more often their successors in ownership, lacked sensitivity to the importance of the harmonious ensemble. One sad example was the Anderton Court Center, constructed in Beverly Hills in the 1950s. Inherently insensitive to Wright's architecture but impressed by his reputation, the client was anticipating a high investment return from the building. The amazing design provided five small shops on a very small urban lot in a highly fashionable retail business street. The shops, all with visible show windows, occupied three levels accessed by ramps.

The leasing arrangements should have included a clause making it mandatory for the shops to have their interior furnishings designed by Wright, thus maintaining their integrity as interesting variations within the organic whole; but no such clause was included. As a result the owner leased each shop to the highest bidder, regardless of the nature of the product, and allowed the lessee full freedom to "decorate" as he or she wished. The result is catastrophic, another example of self-defeating greed. On viewing it, Wright said "I lost this one by default."

The building, incidentally, was an interesting mono-material structural design, using reinforced spray-applied concrete against one form. It was both structurally and economically successful. I set it up to be built without a general contractor, and Wright furnished one of his best apprentices to serve as construction manager. A building permit was obtained only with Wright's personal intervention to charm the building inspection official, who wasn't up to understanding the plans. At least that part of the process was enjoyed by Frank Lloyd Wright in this case.

A large proportion of Wright's buildings were constructed in a hostile environment of ignorance. In most cases building permits were obtained with great difficulty, in some cases ignored entirely; otherwise the construction could not have proceeded. Innovative construction techniques were often ignorantly considered unsafe; many had to be field-tested to convince skeptical building inspectors or structural engineers. The "dendriform" column of the Johnson Administration Building was test-loaded at the site and proved it would support more than six times its required load; the solid wood "Usonian" walls site-tested in various communities proved able to support four times the required load. In Marin County, continuous-arch shell roof slabs supported over twice the design load when tested.

Problems with an unenlightened bureaucracy, which tries to apply formulas still on the books to structural circumstances not anticipated by those formulas, continued to plague Wright's work even after his death. In Marin County, outside engineers called in by building inspection procedures vetoed Wright's articulated structural design for the structure, and thereby lowered its seismic resistance by their insistence on tightly connecting joints that had been designed to be flexible. Wright's design of the Imperial Hotel in Tokyo was also criticized by the engineering profession; but the hotel became one of the few buildings to survive Tokyo's 1923 earthquake, the worst in over a century, thanks to an innovative structure designed to resist seismic forces.

Not only bureaucrats and engineers, but many architects as well, have persisted in ignoring the logic of Wright's architectural philosophy. The tenets that appear to accompany the current "Postmodern" architectural style have been developed primarily by academic architects, a group described by Wright as "intellectuals educated beyond their capacity." This superficial proliferation of a pastiche of unrelated mannerisms plucked from history books and utilized without regard to basic functional concerns, climate, or a natural expression of contemporary materials and techniques is the antithesis of organic architecture. Wright's words here are a synthesis of warning and prophecy:

I suggest that a revival, not of the Gothic style but of the Gothic spirit, is needed in the Art and Architecture of the modern life of the world. We all now need interpretation of the best traditions in the world but made to match the great Tradition and our own individual methods. We must repulse every stupid attempt to imitate and fasten ancient forms, however scientific—upon a life that must outgrow them however great they seem.[6]

But this modern constructive endeavor is being victimized at the start by a certain new aesthetic wherein appearance is made an aim instead of character made a purpose.[7]

Architecture is the very body of civilization itself. It takes time to grow—begins to be architecture only when it is thought-built,—that is to say when it is a synthesis completed from a rational beginning and, naturally as breathing, genuinely modern.[8]

NOTES

1. *College Art Journal,* 6, No. 1 (Autumn 1946), pp. 41–42.
2. From the Preface to *Ausgeführte Bauten und Entwürfe* (Berlin: Wasmuth, 1910), reprinted as *Buildings, Plans and Designs* (New York: Horizon Press, 1963), p. 2.
3. *Ibid.,* p. 9.
4. *The Natural House* (New York: Horizon Press, 1954), p. 23.
5. From the Preface to *Ausgeführte Bauten und Entwürfe,* 1963 reprint (see note 2), p. 11.
6. *Ibid.,* n.p.
7. *The Future of Architecture* (New York: Horizon Press, 1953), p. 211.
8. *Ibid.,* p. 215.

# STRUCTURE IN ORGANIC ARCHITECTURE

*E. T. Casey*

In the latter part of the thirteenth century, a dozen years after their completion, the high vaults of Beauvais Cathedral collapsed. We can easily imagine that those residing nearby must have felt as though the end of the world was at hand. The structure was rebuilt, endured yet another partial collapse and rebuilding in the sixteenth century, and, although never brought to ultimate completion, remains a lasting monument to the skill of masonry construction. It was a daring experiment in architecture in an era subsequently recognized as extraordinary for the fusion of structure and architecture.

Over the succeeding centuries, controversy has accompanied every attempt to analyze the stresses in the many components of complex structures like the Beauvais Cathedral, which were the product of intuition and experience. Only now, in the last half of the twentieth century, are the ingenious techniques of photoelastic analysis beginning to reveal the accuracy of these earlier intuitions.

The collapse of the Beauvais Cathedral has been attributed to the failure of the architect not as an artist but as an engineer, in clear recognition that both functions are essential components of true architecture. This perspective, the combination of artist and engineer, may be useful in examining the organic architecture of Frank Lloyd Wright.

A key to understanding how the components of structure evolved and fused with architecture in Mr. Wright's work is found in the dedication he composed for the introductory panel in the exhibition he entitled "Sixty Years of Living Architecture": "In the realm of ideas, to you: this record of patient research and genuine experiment according to experience, faithful to the nature of whatever was being done." Experiment is the guiding principle at work: true experiment, defined as a steady evolution or building of experience, each manifestation built on the lessons of the past; "learning by doing"; the favorite project always the next one. Wright's work was truly experimental, as opposed to experimental in the sense of novel or capricious, different for the sake of appearances only. He searched for concepts of structure in a tree as well as a seashell, in a study of Gothic cathedrals as well as the latest technology of new materials. Over a career spanning seven decades and a thousand designs, he fused imaginative concepts of structure with imaginative uses of materials to create and articulate a new vocabulary of spaces suitable to humanity in the present and the future.

Edmond Thomas Casey took his B.A. in Architecture from the University of California, Berkeley. He is a Registered Architect and a Professional (Structural) Engineer. He represented the Wright firm in Iran for a number of years in the 1970s, planning and directing architectural projects. He is a member of the Board of Trustees of the Frank Lloyd Wright Foundation, and Director of Education of the Frank Lloyd Wright School of Architecture.

In the late nineteenth century and the beginning of the twentieth, the technology of building construction changed very rapidly in comparison to previous eras. The advent of the industrial revolution introduced new materials that would affect all building in the future. Masonry, the most enduring construction method of former times, relied on weight to direct all loads to the earth. If we think of all loads generating either push or pull, i.e. compression or tension, then we may say that the masonry construction of earlier times could resist push but not pull, since masonry is relatively weak in tensile strength. Steel and concrete, the new materials of construction now available during this period, could be arranged to transmit both push and pull with equal strength. This change in the strength of materials, coupled with the application of a growing scientific understanding of the physical laws of nature, is the basis of modern construction technology.

Like the builders of Gothic cathedrals, Frank Lloyd Wright had an intuitive grasp of how to integrate architectural expression with a pragmatic structural concept. This intuition was the result of a lifelong curiosity and absorption with the study of the "nature" of things: nature not so much in the sense of flora and fauna, but in the sense of the message of the structure of growth forms capable of expression as essence. He often referred to nature with a capital N as the church he attended for spiritual refreshment and strength. Thus he tells of his observation that trees with taproots survived violent windstorms while those without taproots were frequently blown over. The application: the use of a deep vertical foundation as the most effective way of fortifying tall buildings against the overturning forces of wind or earthquake. In a similar fashion, the analogy of limbs of a tree cantilevered from the trunk led him to treat the floors of a building in the same manner,

with all forces transferred to a vertical core and thence to the earth.

Wright's Imperial Hotel in Tokyo was one of only a few buildings to survive the great earthquake of 1923. Thanks to the continuity of its floors with a central core of walls, divided into segments approximately 60 feet long, all resting on foundations supported on friction piles, the building was adequately flexible to absorb the wave of ground motion. Decades later the application of this principle of flexibility and dynamic response created a major advance in the design of tall buildings subject to seismic forces.

Subsequently refined by analytical development, this same idea became a major component of lateral-force-resisting systems for multistoried buildings. In this application, walls are no longer necessary as principal elements of support and are thus free to become screens or curtains only, to separate outdoors from indoors. Frank Lloyd Wright's designs for multistoried tall buildings, from the glass curtain wall of the Luxfer Prism Company Building of 1895 to the mile-high mast of the Illinois project of 1956, all reflect this technological development.

Wright never stopped thinking about ways of making buildings earthquake-proof. In the early stages of development of his design for the Guggenheim Museum, he imagined that the spiral ramp might be constructed as a giant coil spring. In his inimitable way, with a twinkle in his eye, he remarked how effective that could be: "If there were an earthquake, the building would simply bounce down the street, no harm done!" As finally designed, of course, the ramp does not act as a spring; but only a truly superior architectural imagination could have come up with such an idea.

The desert cacti of the southwest were another source of inspiration for efficient structures. The tall, slender saguaro, strengthened by vertical reinforcing ribs evenly distributed around its perimeter, is capable of supporting and storing tons of moisture over the centuries of its life-span. The staghorn and cholla cacti reveal a tubular lattice limb structure of exceptional strength with a minimum amount of material. All desert plant life, in fact, illustrates the maximum use of a minimum of substance to sustain life with a character and beauty particularly expressive of its severe environment.

In direct application of this observation, Wright used an expanded steel-mesh reinforcement in the concrete walls of the hollow dendriform columns of the Johnson Wax Building in Racine, Wisconsin, in 1936. The test of the ultimate strength of the column became one of the more widely publicized triumphs of his intuitive applications over codified regulation. The column defied the conventional wisdom of the time by being larger at the top than at the base, hollow in its shaft, and otherwise beyond the limits of conventional calculation. A load test convincingly demonstrated that the column was capable of carrying more than five times the load specified in the code.

In addition to structural applications, the notion of "genuine experiment" included the consideration of new kinds of materials, including easily available materials that were scorned by contemporary architects. Poured concrete and the concrete block are two notable examples. In the early decades of the twentieth century, both plain concrete and reinforced concrete were generally considered too ugly to use as a finished surface despite concrete's great strength, longevity, and plastic properties. In Unity Temple, built in Oak Park, Illinois, in 1904, Wright showed what could be done with concrete. The gravel aggregate of the concrete itself was exposed to form the finished surface of the building, replacing the conventional stone or brick facing and saving expense. In the decades since this early pioneering effort, exposed aggregate has become one of the most enduring finishes of architectural concrete.

As early as 1906 Wright began to experiment with the concrete block, which at the time was used only as a back-up material or in the most utilitarian of structures. His high regard for this simple and inexpensive material lasted for the rest of his life, being expressed notably in his "textile block system" residences of the twenties and his Usonian Automatic block system developed in the fifties. Perhaps no material held more promise than the concrete block for translating into reality Wright's conclusion that the strength of the democratic system depended on the independent stake of each individual in the system—each family in its own home on its own ground. The contribution of the architect to this goal was the invention of a system of construction that would make it possible for even a family of the most modest means to build its own house. The prefabricated housing of Broadacre City, the wooden Usonian kit houses, the All-Steel housing development proposal, and the concrete-block Usonian Automatic houses were all efforts to this end.

Wright's goal in the present and hope for the future was the development of the true society of democracy as expressed in the Declaration of Independence, the Constitution, and the political organization of the electorate. For these civilizing arrangements to evolve to the level of a sustaining culture, he thought, their meaning must also find expression in architecture in a combination of technology and materials similar to the achievements of the Gothic era.

At the dawn of the twentieth century the technology and materials were at hand. The machine was the artist's new tool:

the question was how best to use it. During his apprenticeship to Louis Sullivan and under his tutelage Wright had achieved an extraordinary skill in free-hand drawing and architectural drafting, as surviving drawings attest, but he soon gave up free-hand drawing in favor of the T-square and triangle as more in keeping with the requirements of machine-made technology. Similarly, he experimented with repetitive motifs in decorative elements, which the machine could reproduce with great regularity at a great economy of labor.

In due course the idea of construction by machine evolved into the idea of having pre-cut parts made in a factory and shipped to distant sites to be assembled into a house. The American System Ready-cut Houses of 1911 were one expression of this idea. Another was the Usonian House, which was developed during and in response to the Great Depression.

Many innovations in construction technology were involved in the Usonian House. The foundation and floor were combined in a single concrete slab. The roof was conceived as a monolithic plane bound together around the perimeter by a continuous band or header, which replaced the header capping all walls in the familiar balloon framing system of carpentry. This roof plane was supported by a combination of masonry piers or rectangular masses and vertical mullions, allowing the walls to become screens of glazed sash or wood panels composed of boards and battens fastened to a plywood core. The system of assembly was designed to reduce the amount of work in the field. After the floor slab was in place, the roof was built and supported using the minimum of vertical supports. The remainder of the enclosure was then put in place, under the protection of the roof, using as far as possible pre-assembled, prefinished elements manufactured in a mill or factory.

The Usonian House exemplifies the flow of ideas that led to buildings by Frank Lloyd Wright. To understand this kind of thinking we must look beyond a formal engineering analysis of the forces involved, and beyond structure in the sense of individual exposed members with clean, simple, smooth joints. The structural form we are seeking is a subjective one, one that expresses the purpose being served in terms of the nature of the materials employed.

In the early decades Wright's engineering of forms was intuitive, and in the case of some larger unbuilt projects extraordinarily imaginative. Among the built projects many appeared to defy conventional calculation methods common to buildings. However, as his experiment in organic architecture progressed and his forms grew more daring in concept, particularly in reinforced concrete, rational analysis developed in other engineered constructions became available. Thus, for example, advances in aircraft design that made possible lighter, stronger constructions produced analytic procedures readily adapted to building construction, although in many cases these were very slow to be accepted by building code authorities.

A particularly important early example of the fusion of form, function, materials, and methods of construction is the windmill tower called Romeo and Juliet at Hillside near Taliesin in Wisconsin, built in 1896. This tower served as a wind-driven water pump and also as a lookout tower, being located on top of a prominent hill overlooking the entire farm. The tower is constructed as a closed octagonal tube joined to a diamond-shaped tube whose point is oriented toward the prevailing wind direction. These vertical tubes are stiffened by horizontal diaphragm "floors" occurring regularly throughout the tower's height.

By the 1930s, when the Kaufmann "Fallingwater" residence and the S. C. Johnson Administration Building were built, rational methods of structural analysis were available for application to reinforced concrete, particularly when it was used as a homogeneous plastic material capable of withstanding large tensile as well as compressive stresses. A building could be made to accept as much pull as push, and the cantilever was the form that expressed this possibility in the most dramatic fashion, combining leanness or spareness with grace and good proportion to produce a sense of elegant slenderness.

The continuity of the cantilever allowed support to be displaced from the corner, the traditional position associated with vertical support. Formerly spaces for habitation were defined by supporting corners, becoming in effect boxes stacked horizontally and/or vertically together. If support was no longer confined to the corner, what better way to free the space than to open the corner by replacing it with glass, "air in air to keep air in and keep air out"? Thus the corner window became an appropriate symbol of the destruction of the box.

In retrospect the evolution appears obvious, but in fact it took the form of a steady succession of patient experiments driven by intuition and artistic inspiration. Gradually the liberation of space by the destruction of the box became the architectonic depiction of the liberation of the individual, the sovereign of his or her particular space.

In 1947 Wright designed a bridge to be made of reinforced concrete. He called it the Butterfly Bridge, the name being derived from the appearance of the cross-section. Roadways were cantilevered from each side of a central concrete girder that spanned between piers spaced eighty feet apart. The cantilevered forms were hollow; thin concrete slabs formed the top and bottom surfaces. The vertical depth at the face of the girder tapered to a thin horizontal edge, while the girder arched from pier to pier. These curved shell-like forms were particularly suited to the use of concrete and added strength and stability as well as a graceful shape, especially when compared to the shape of steel truss bridges built above the roadway, which were common at that time. In this bridge design, structure and architectural expression are inseparable. Wright's proposal for a second crossing of San Francisco Bay in 1949 was a direct development from the Butterfly Bridge design.

In contrast to the reinforced concrete bridge, the steel suspension bridges of the Pittsburgh Point project, designed in 1948, exploited the unique strength of steel in tension—in Wright's words, "the spider spinning." The steel bridge designs derived from a concept of structure different from the concrete bridge designs, and the resulting architectural expression was altogether different, although their function was nearly identical. The graceful cable fans of the new Sunshine Skyway bridge across lower Tampa Bay in Florida embody the thrilling and majestic structure proposed decades earlier for Pittsburgh.

Of course, concrete may be made to perform as lumber; of course, steel may be shaped in many forms. But all too many uses of these materials sell them short. The search of an organic architecture is for expression of the unique qualities of materials as definitions of spaces. Too few people yet understand that the freedom Wright pursued was always founded on sound structural principles, that he combined in his work all the quality of American engineering technology with the artistry of a poet of materials.

To this day, what with the ever-increasing specialization of contemporary professions, many architects can only conceive a building as a decorated facade, leaving the structure, from which the architecture should grow, to the engineers to work out. Rather than a synthesis of architecture and structure, we have a dichotomy or even an adversary relationship. This was one of the chief problems Frank Lloyd Wright addressed when he gave us a new way to think about buildings. It is still to be hoped that his ideas will prevail with American architects and those for whom they design.

# FRANK LLOYD WRIGHT'S CONCEPT OF DEMOCRACY: AN AMERICAN ARCHITECTURAL JEREMIAD

*Narciso G. Menocal*

During his last thirty years Frank Lloyd Wright became increasingly insistent on the relationship between architecture and democracy, writing extensively on the subject.[1] This study seeks to describe that relationship. Within this context, I wish to link Wright's concept of architecture to the American tradition of the jeremiad; to propose that he twice expanded the scope of that concept (at the turn of the century and from the late 1920s through the mid-1930s); and to argue that the concept remained unchanged throughout his life, although he enhanced it in his sixties.

My concern is Wright's concept of architecture, not the characteristics that collectively shape what is known as "the Wrightian style." For that concern it becomes necessary to distinguish between *concept* and *conception* of architecture. The concept is an idea that is basic, indwelling, and elemental to the point of lacking in parts. A conception is the opposite. It is a derived phenomenon, visible, tangible, and complex. Whereas the concept exists only as an abstraction, the con-

ception stands in time and space, and in the shape of a specific design evolves from one project to the next. The concept remains unchanged during this evolution. Once an architect formulates a concept, it remains perpetually stable, but the architect's own understanding of it, and of the possibilities it offers, does not. There will be occasional flashes of deep intuition and periods of stable growth, but there will also be stretches when the realization of the concept does not change.

I shall deal with only a few major sources of Wright's concept of architecture: Whitman, Victor Hugo, Viollet-le-Duc, music, Edward Bellamy, Henry George, Silvio Gesell, and the architect's own Lloyd-Jones family background. Japanese prints, Froebel blocks, the Vienna Secession, Pure Design, and the like had more to do with shaping Wright's style than with helping him arrive at a concept of architecture. For the present purpose they are of peripheral interest.

One last prefatory remark concerns the term *jeremiad*. I am not using it in its standard meaning (as stated in the *Oxford English Dictionary*) of "a lamentation; a writing or speech in a strain of grief or distress; a doleful complaint; a complaining tirade; a lugubrious effusion." That meaning refers to the lamentations of the prophet Jeremiah over the loss of Jerusalem to the Babylonians. The side of the jeremiad relevant to this essay

Narciso G. Menocal studied in Quebec and Havana before taking his Bachelor of Architecture and M.A. (Arch.) degrees from the University of Florida. He received his Ph.D. in Art History from the University of Illinois. He is Professor and Chairman of the Department of Art History, University of Wisconsin at Madison. An authority on the work of Louis Sullivan, he is beginning to publish widely on the work of Frank Lloyd Wright.

is another. It bears upon the prophet's concern with whether the Israelites, in captivity, would keep their covenant with Jehovah. It was in this covenant that their identity lay, and it was through this covenant that they became morally superior to all other nations. I use the word *jeremiad* in this latter sense to signify a covenant with a higher order—divine or natural— for the purposes of attaining to perfection, or to the utopia.

Surprisingly, Frank Lloyd Wright has never been overtly identified with the jeremiad, that quintessentially American dictum that promises utopia to those who embrace nature after stepping out of history and tradition. Yet Wright's architecture, as well as his political and social *personae,* suggests such a consideration.[2] Broadacre City (his plan for the architectural redefinition of the nation as a conglomerate of quasi-rural counties) would have depended for success on a national consensus intrinsic to the meaning of mandate, implicit in the notion of controlled process, and central to the American vision of union through multiplicity.

The jeremiad, although first established as a national ritual during the Federalist and Jacksonian eras, had its sources in the so-called "political sermons" of the Puritans and in subsequent eighteenth-century adaptations of Puritan rhetoric, especially during the Great Awakening.[3] It has been argued that after the Puritans established a covenant with God, the Enlightenment re-established it with nature, a redefinition that "freed [the new Republic] from the burdens of European history as long as its citizens avoided the creation of complexity."[4] Like the prophet of old reminding the children of Israel to keep the faith among the Babylonians, American Jeremiahs preached the need to live according to an eternal and immutable ideal established by nature, one that in the end would defeat the artificiality of the traditions of humankind, on which rested the tyranny of history.

After the American Revolution "the holy commonwealth spread westward across the continent, bringing light into darkness; the frontier movement came to provide a sort of serial enactment of the ritual of the jeremiad."[5] Giving voice to a myth based partly on chauvinism and partly on eschatology, the jeremiad helped to create nineteenth-century nationwide visions of "the city on the hill," of "God's American Israel," of "America, the New Garden of Eden," or simply of "God's country," where the covenant with nature would be finally realized for the fulfillment of humanity.[6] Thus the words of the prophet would come to pass: "This shall be the covenant that I will make with the house of Israel. . . . I will put my law in their inward parts, and write it in their hearts; and will be their God, and they shall be my people. And they shall teach no more every man his neighbour, and every man his brother, saying, Know the Lord: for they shall all know Me, from the least of them unto the greatest of them."[7] Patently, nature as a transcendent force had replaced Jehovah by the nineteenth century.

Much American literature of the Jacksonian and Antebellum periods shares characteristics with the jeremiad, and Whitman's concept of democracy is especially important to understanding Frank Lloyd Wright. Whitman's notion that "the true idea of Nature" was central to democracy; his belief that "true democracy" would be "warranting results like those of Nature's laws, reliable, when once establish'd, to carry on themselves"; his ideas on the superiority of individualism over collectivisim ("the significant wonders of heaven and earth

[are] significant only because of the Me in the centre"); and his belief that individualism "has been the political genesis of America," and will finally "make this American world see that it is the final authority and reliance," are notions that Wright, and his Lloyd-Jones family, shared to a greater or lesser degree.[8] But to Whitman (and later to Wright), democracy had not yet been established in the land. As Whitman put it, "Feudalism, caste, the ecclesiastical traditions, though palpably retreating from political institutions, still hold essentially, by their spirit, even in this country, entire possession of the more important fields, indeed the very subsoil, of education, and of social standards and literature."[9] Finally, to both Whitman and Wright, "democracy can never prove itself beyond cavil, until it founds and luxuriantly grows its own forms of art, poems, schools, theology, displacing all that exists, or that has been produced anywhere in the past, under opposite influences."[10]

This tradition, in a household where "one's mother, father, aunts, and uncles were always quoting: 'As Mr. Emerson says . . .,'"[11] served as a foundation for many of Wright's later ideas, for by the time of his parents' generation the rhetorical devices of the jeremiad were conventions of cultural self-definition. The family motto, "Truth against the World," although of Welsh origin, had much in common with the intrinsically American reliance on innate natural instincts and with the belief that these instincts, because they are natural, are superior to knowledge handed down by historical tradition based on "autocratic" European antecedents.

Wright always fitted European notions into an American mold, and he adapted European architectural theory to the jeremiad. His transformation of ideas of Victor Hugo and of Viollet-le-Duc into his own exemplifies that tendency. When as a young man in Chicago Wright read *Notre-Dame de Paris*, he became enthralled with Victor Hugo's conception of architecture. According to Hugo, in the Middle Ages "whoever was born a poet became an architect" and imbued buildings with hidden and overt symbols holding the key to absolute knowledge.[12] The presence of these symbols, in turn, compelled each subsequent generation of scholars to seek for adumbrations of the mysteries lurking behind the beauty of architecture.[13] But from the moment the printing press began to transmit knowledge to increasingly wider circles of readers, it was no longer convenient—in fact, it became impossible—to couch universal knowledge in terms of mystery and symbols. The price of the clarity of the printed word was the loss of poetry of architecture.

The buildings of the Renaissance, "of that setting sun Europe mistook for dawn," became dry exercises in erudition on the classical orders. Eventually "architecture crawled like a pitiful beggar of the studios, from copy to copy of the Greek, Roman, and barbaric works of professors according to Vitruvius and Vignola."[14] Under these circumstances architecture could only serve as a witness to the passage of time; the book of architecture, no longer preserving universal mysteries, would become a mere chronicle.[15] Wright agreed with Hugo that in medieval buildings form, function, construction, and meaning had been brought together more harmoniously than at any other time. Wright, in fact, "conceived and worked to conclusion [his architecture] in the Gothic spirit";[16] yet he proceeded to bend the argument to an American, modern, and utopian point of view. In the end, he disproved Hugo's fundamental point.

To Hugo, the message of architecture was to be based on the

*Hermetica*—that is, on the corpus of knowledge sages had assembled in the process of unraveling the mysteries of the universe, which they expressed in arcane symbols. To Wright, architecture was to be a celebration of the joy of nature for everyone's delight. Hugo looked at the past and was awed by it; the modern architect, at best, could only hope to imitate how the Middle Ages had brought together architecture and learning. Hugo's view was revivalist, subservient, and therefore traditional. The machine, the modern monster (represented in the fifteenth century by the printing press), had destroyed the possibility for architecture to become once more "hermetical." Wright saw it differently. By mastering the machine rather than letting the machine master it, humanity could once more make architecture the premier among the arts, the one that "allows for a new beginning"[17] and that expresses most clearly the essence and secret of nature.

Viollet-le-Duc helped Wright establish that direct relationship between architecture and nature.[18] For Viollet there existed a higher logical order that structured all natural creations. One of the important functions of human intelligence was to discover such an order and apply its principles in human creation, including architecture. How nature regulated the outward appearance of animals, plants, and minerals was the basis of architecture as well as of all design. Applying this natural principle generated *style,* "the manifestation of an ideal established on a principle."[19] Through the most logical use of materials and of methods of construction a building (or any other human creation) was to express with the greatest economy—and on first impression—its character, its uses, and how efficiently it served its purpose. In this respect Viollet wrote in his *Discourses on Architecture*:

The lilies of the field, the leaves of the trees, the insects, have style, because they grow, develop, and exist according to essential logical laws. We can spare nothing from a flower because, in its organization, every part has its function and is formed to carry out that function in the most beautiful manner. Style resides in the true and well-understood expression of a principle, everything must have style.[20]

Wright paraphrased this passage at least three times; in the preface to *Ausgeführte Bauten und Entwürfe,* for example, he states:

What is Style?—Every flower has it, every animal too; every individual worthy of the name has style in some degree. . . . An harmonious entity of whatever sort in its entirety cannot fail of style in the best sense.[21]

Geometric simplification was one of Wright's most useful tools for establishing what he and Viollet considered to be "a sense of style." To Viollet there had to be a tight correlation between architectural proportion and the geometry of the granite rhomboids that structured the crust of the earth. One issued out of the other and both were extensions of the framework underlying the universal order.[22] Since each rhomboid was formed from interlocking pyramids—each defined in turn by four equilateral triangles—nature's "wisdom" was made apparent in her choice of this most stable of shapes to prevent the internal energy of planets from bursting out. It was this kind of "natural" reasoning that architects were to apply to constructing sound and stable buildings.[23] The lesson in economy became complete when Viollet pointed out that the proportions of the equilateral triangle were pleasing because they are rational. His next step was to propose a universal system of architectural proportion based on triangulation to make architecture an extension of nature. The Middle Ages had established such a relationship, as he asserted in both the *Dictionnaire* and the *Discourses*.[24]

Early in his career Wright also developed a modular method of proportion, but his was based at first on the square. (Later he would add the rectangle, the triangle, the hexagon, and the circle, as well as combinations of these shapes.) Wright's system depended not on a geomorphic conceit, but on the spanning capability of materials. At the same time it related the building to the site. More important, in subtle ways his modular system linked his architecture to a universal, Pythagorean rhythm. In his *Autobiography* Wright referred to "planned progressions, thematic evolutions, the never-ending variety in differentiation of pattern [and to] integral ornament always belonging naturally enough to the simplest statement of the prime idea upon which the superstructure is based."[25] This statement linked the modular characteristics and overall sense of composition of architecture to similar traits of music.

Instead of searching for rhythms in the structure of matter, as Viollet did, Wright opted for a higher level: "The symphony, as my father first taught me, is an edifice of sound. Just as I now feel that architecture ought to be symphonic."[26] Developing that idea, he stated, "There is a similarity of vision in creation between Music and Architecture. Only the nature of the materials differs."[27] At another time he explained that "music and architecture blossom on the same stem: sublimated mathematics. Mathematics as presented by geometry. Instead of the musician's systematic staff and intervals, the architect has a modular system as the framework of design."[28] Wright's architecture—or "mathematics in co-ordinated Form" as he once defined it[29]—uses a system that operates like that of music, in which rhythm brings order to the sounds exe-cuted within a measure, and the rhythm, in turn, is established by ratios that either double or halve the length of a sound.[30]

This similarity between music and Wright's work implies a belief that a shape of a given size within a design—the module—serves the purpose of both a full note and the length of a bar. This system allows for an almost infinite number of combinations through arithmetical and geometrical manipulation in which the parts always stand in harmonic relationship to each other as well as to the whole. By declaring that "the differentiation of a single, certain form characterizes the expression of one building [and] quite a different form may serve for another, but from a basic idea all the formal elements of design are in each case derived and held together in scale and character," Wright revealed his belief in the existence of one salient feature that varied from design to design but that nevertheless gave each building its peculiar character.[31]

Neither this feature nor the geometric basis of a design was to be revealed obviously. Ideally, the plan determined the materials; the materials dictated the methods of construction; the methods of construction established the scale and the proportions of the module; and the proportions generated the articulation.[32] These elements, together and by themselves, were to produce the style of the building seemingly without the active participation of the architect, just as nature had determined the *style* of Viollet's flower and insect.

Viollet's method produced a lackluster architecture because he applied his system mechanically, as an end; Wright, by contrast, used the module as a means, holding that "geometry is to Architecture only what mathematics is to Music."[33] There was a further dimension that Viollet had disregarded; Wright called it a "Reality [that] is supergeometric, casting a spell or 'charm' over the obvious[ly] geometric."[34] The building had to obey the strict discipline of geometry, but the composition had to be as seemingly free as those of nature. Everything should be "especially designed to be perfectly natural to itself . . . as sheep, crows, and butterflies are out of doors," yet "nothing is so severe a strain [on the artist] as this discipline from within."[35]

Architecture, like any other entity in nature, was to signify only itself. At most its metaphorical value was to stand for a way of life Wright called "democratic"—that is, based on principles of nature. His buildings were to create the illusion that they were "organic." For Wright architectural forms— and hence forms depending on geometry—grew from the tectonic essence of the earth and transformed themselves into a building not by accretion, but through interpenetration, through a process of continuous generation that made one space issue from the preceding one. This process never came to an end; it constantly turned in on itself, or onto the landscape, or onto both.

In that process lies the meaning of Wright's concept of the democratic, and hence of the organic, for to him the two words were synonymous, signifying a harmony with nature. In his architecture there was growth and there was life, in that nature created the building. In the end he was but an agent of nature, the source of all that exists. The architect, at best, was the one whose talent imparted to the design that "super-geometric Reality" without which all architecture is colorless and inorganic. Wright's knowledge of Pure Design, the Vienna Secession, the Froebel kindergarten toys, and the like, together with his personal interpretation of the Japanese print, allowed him to create his style as an extension of what he saw as nature's style. Familiarity with those entities also helped him to express the particular character of a building. He never forgot that each specimen in nature is unique in appearance. At the same time his system of architecture—and consequently his idea of it—echoed the basic geometric order and rhythm sustaining the universe.[36] The mystery of the *hermetica* lay for Wright in that relationship of nature and architecture, both expressing the same truth. By making that secret public through his work, Wright had two aims, one resulting from the other: to create the architecture required by a Whitmanesque, utopian democracy, and hence to restore architecture to its rightful premier position among the arts, the position it had occupied during the Middle Ages.

In general, these were the limits of the "democratic content" of Wright's architecture from the early Prairie years through the mid-1920s. By extending Viollet's rational principles into a position diametrically opposed to Hugo's, Wright defined a concept of architecture that sought the characteristic in an organic sense. He believed that every person should realize that the individual existed as part of nature. Concurrently, everything in nature mirrors his or her existence. This symmetry was for Wright the basis of the covenant of democracy. An organic architecture, as he defined it, was to him the only truly democratic one, since no other could accommodate the covenant between humankind and nature. That covenant was ambivalent in that it was universal, yet fostered individualism. Much of the beauty in his work depends on his having established this fundamental romantic tension between the ideal and the characteristic, a polarity that allowed for a constantly changing conception of architecture while the concept of it remained invariable. This resulted in works that are totally consistent with his unifying concept of architecture, but that are as stylistically different from each other as the Willitts House, the Imperial Hotel, La Miniatura, the Usonian houses, and the Mile High Illinois skyscraper.

Wright's concept of architecture expanded during the late 1920s and early 1930s. During the first three decades of his career he had shown more concern for the relationship of his architecture to nature than for the relationship of his buildings to society at large. Seldom did he work on planning problems on a scale larger than that of the individual building. The Quadruple Houses (1901), the Como Orchard Summer Colony (1909–10), the "Non-Competitive Plan" for the National Conference on City Planning (1913), the Doheny Ranch project (1921), and the Lake Tahoe Summer Colony (1922) may come to mind as multiple building projects, but none of them addressed the problems of the city as a whole.[37] Neither do Wright's writings from before 1930 show much concern with social problems or with their architectural solutions.

Social awareness came when circumstances forced him to redefine his values to overcome that difficult period in his life that began with his liaison with Olgivanna Milanoff, who eventually became his third wife.[38] She was a source of strength during those years when his second wife, Miriam Noel, refused to grant him a divorce, and at one point had him committed to jail in Minnesota for violating the Mann Act. During that period, Taliesin burned down for the second time, Wright's collection of Japanese prints was auctioned publicly (followed by his farm equipment and household goods), and he was plagued by sensationalism and notoriety. Partly to assuage his emotional burdens, and partly to help him reestablish the professional status that had been tarnished by

personal imbroglios, Olgivanna Wright did two things: she encouraged him to write at length to redefine his position in architecture, and she urged him to take strength from his Lloyd-Jones heritage.[39]

Wright's written oeuvre of this period began with the nine articles titled "In the Cause of Architecture," published in 1928 in the *Architectural Record*. The articles cover such subjects as the constituents of architecture, the modular nature of the plan, the meaning of *style*, the use of materials, and, in the last article in the series, the terms of architecture. In 1931 Princeton University Press published his Kahn Lectures of the preceding year, in which he once more defined his position in modern architecture. His *Autobiography*, which he had begun writing in 1927, appeared in 1932, the same year that he dealt for the first time with the relationship of architecture to society at large in *The Disappearing City*. In this second book Wright called for a decentralized, agrarian society based on what he considered to be the proper use of the machine and of national resources. This was the beginning of Broadacre City as an idea, and of the Taliesin Fellowship.

Wright issued his own jeremiad during this period, almost as a catharsis. Taliesin, his architectural self-portrait, was in his mind as one with Jones Valley, the place that he identified with and that he considered to be the land of his ancestors—although the valley had become family property only a year before his birth.[40] As far as Wright was concerned, his "ancestry" was only two generations deep, for he made his grandparents the first characters in the canonical myth that a jeremiad required. Like the Pilgrims of old, Richard Jones and Mary Lloyd had come to the New World seeking religious freedom. They were paragons of virtue: true, upright, honest, and hardworking. Shunning the wicked ways of the city and enduring innumerable hardships, including the death of a child, they finally made their way to the beautiful valley in remote Wisconsin, where like a new Abraham and Sarah arriving in Canaan, they found their reward through a covenant with nature. Their strength of character and understanding of nature allowed them to build a haven for themselves in surroundings where their motto, "Truth against the World," was once and for all at home—neither arrogant nor out of place—because the valley itself avouched such ideas.

The family worked in unison for the same purposeful errand. Richard, the patriarch, and his sons, like bearded biblical figures, shaped the valley into their own image. Richard's daughters Jane and Nell, overlooking the valley from their Hillside Home School, spread to the young a gospel of symbiosis with the land. Their brother Jenkin, one of the most prominent Unitarian ministers in the nation, proclaimed similar ideas to ever-widening circles. Daughter Anna, separated by marriage from the clan, zealously instilled the family values in her son Frank.

The message this information implies is clear in Wright's *Autobiography*. In that document the architect set his ancestors and their holdings within the tradition of the American jeremiad (the oldest and most essential of all national traditions). By so doing he implied that they belonged more on the mythical than on the temporal level and turned their arrival in America almost into a hierophany. In Wright's version, "the city on the hill" had been established by his family by the time he was a child. All he had to do was to reshape it in his image and—in his opinion—offer it as an architectural solution to all the ills of the world.[41] By the late 1920s he had become determined to turn his work into an expression of the American ethos, as he understood it in terms of his family heritage, which he now extolled in print to complete a cycle. He also realized that because that heritage existed outside of time, it was not subject to the vagaries of history. It was invested with the archetypal force of myth.

But before he could translate his jeremiad into buildings, he needed to create a team to assist him in giving his idea a tangible architectural shape. It was to this end that Olgivanna Wright conceived of the Taliesin Fellowship. The Hillside Home School buildings, empty since 1917 and deteriorated, remained a symbol of what Wright considered best in the Lloyd-Jones clan. His wife urged him to revive and expand the family tradition, or better, the family calling. By 1930, as historian Robert Twombly has noted, Wright was pointing out in his Princeton lectures how America's creative energies could be developed by means of "industrial style centers." Under the direction of master craftsmen, forty students at each center would study glassmaking, pottery, textiles, sheet metal, woodworking, dance, music, or another art for seven hours a day. For another three they would work on the land to make their center self-sufficient.[42]

On October 1, 1932, the Taliesin Fellowship, "a little experiment station in an out of the way place" (a phrase Wright had used when he had proposed the industrial-style centers at Princeton),[43] was instituted with twenty-three apprentices.[44] In that same month, Wright sought forty workmen from the countryside to refurbish the Hillside Home School buildings and turn them into the Foundation quarters. In the midst of the Depression these men worked for room, board, and one-third of their usual wages, the balance to be paid when the buildings were finished and when "increased apprenticeship fees could be obtained."[45] Apprentices may have thought they were coming to Taliesin to learn architecture in the standard manner, but they found they spent most of their time doing farm labor, working on construction, drafting for Wright, and building his models. As Wright stated, "The Taliesin Fellowship is a 'work' of individual apprentices co-operating and co-ordinating like fingers on my hand. . . . Apprenticeship at Taliesin is much where it was in feudal times, with this important difference: an apprentice then was his master's slave; at Taliesin he is his master's comrade, to the extent he qualifies himself."[46]

Mrs. Wright supervised all the nonarchitectural aspects of the Fellowship. In the rules she instituted, and in the highly structured life she set out for the apprentices, Twombly has seen a similarity with Gurdjieff's Institute for the Harmonious Development of Man in Fontainebleau, where for four years Mrs. Wright had been first a pupil and then an instructor, and where strenuous work was a means to self-discovery. Wright endorsed his wife's interest in Gurdjieff's methods and called Gurdjieff "an organic man . . . [who has] the stuff in him of which our genuine prophets have been made."[47] As at Fontainebleau, where Gurdjieff reigned supreme, there was but one master at Taliesin, rather than the seven Wright had proposed in the Princeton lectures. That master had a vision in need of physical expression, one that encompassed a county, the nation, and presumably also the world.

Broadacre City was Wright's clearest expression of his architectural jeremiad. Consisting of a model of a four-mile-square section of a nation given extraordinary mobility by the automobile, Broadacres showed how 1,400 families could live in sixteen square miles. This project was to represent but one of the units into which the United States was to be recomposed as *Usonia,* with the county as the only unit of government. Each county would become virtually self-sufficient through a combination of light industry and agriculture, and families would live in rural surroundings, each owning a minimum of one acre. Each county would be accessible from a two-tier main arterial road (ten car lanes above and two truck lanes and continuous warehousing below). A high-speed monorail would run above the median. Industry, markets, and motels would be close to this arterial road. Owner-run light industry, workers' housing, and vineyards and orchards would establish a second belt, and a central area would be devoted to "minimum, medium, and larger" houses and three schools. An interdenominational "community church," a university, a zoo, an aquarium, an arboretum, an airport, an arts building, the county seat, the county fair grounds, sports fields, and other ancillary facilities completed the design. Each county would have a population density of about one person per acre, and most of the population would live on small farms. For those with no taste for agriculture, tall apartment buildings would rise from the landscape here and there to establish a correlation between the life of an industrial worker and the countryside. This relationship had its counterpart in the expectation that each farmer would do part-time work in one of the small factories nearby. As Norris Kelly Smith has noted, "what Wright sought to define was a new kind of city, in which the formal opposition of city and country would be eliminated and all the benefits of both city and country life made available to everyone."[48]

Ideas that Edward Bellamy had put forth in his novels *Look-*

*ing Backward* and *Equality* helped Wright to define Broad-acre City. Bellamy (1850–1898), an author better known from the 1890s through the 1930s than he is today, was the son of an impecunious Baptist minister of good New England family. At 18, while studying for a year in Germany, he realized the harshness of life of the urban poor. On his return he became a journalist and a free-lance writer, and his early essays and stories criticized conventional America in a manner reminiscent of Nathaniel Hawthorne.

Bellamy's fame rests mainly on *Looking Backward* (1888), a novel with a simple plot that enabled the author to advance his vision of utopia. Julian West, a wealthy Bostonian, falls into a trance-induced sleep in 1887; waking up in the year 2000, he finds Boston transformed into a lovely and harmonious city. His host, Dr. Leete, introduces him gradually to a new, perfect society where all the ills of old have been corrected and have come to be regarded as curious and stupid idiosyncrasies of only antiquarian interest. Money as such does not exist; everyone is awarded the same amount of yearly credit because everyone works to the best of his abilities; greed and social inequality are things of the past. West adapts quickly to this new and utterly perfect world, and at the end of the novel he is about to marry and settle down, totally assimilated to his new surroundings.

Bellamy's tale of human possibilities was widely read in the United States and abroad. In England, Ebenezer Howard read it at one sitting and was "fairly carried away"; in this country Thorstein Veblen and John Dewey were touched by it.[49] According to Arthur Lewis, a scholar who has devoted much of his work to the study of utopian literature, "The success of the novel was immediate. In the first year there were sales of 60,000

and in the following year over 100,000 as well as translations into French and German, and editions in England. By January of 1891 the book had sold almost 371,000 copies. By the time the sequel, *Equality*, appeared in 1897, over 400,000 copies had been sold in the United States, another 250,000 in England, and a great many in numerous translations. By the mid-90s *Looking Backward* had actually sold more copies than any other American work except *Uncle Tom's Cabin* and *Ben Hur*, records unsurpassed until the mid-20th century."[50] So successful was *Looking Backward* that at least seventeen novels were written to complete its story, dispute its argument, or merely imitate it. Of these, thirteen were published in the United States, one in Germany, another in Canada, and two in England, including William Morris's celebrated *News from Nowhere*. Fifteen of these novels appeared between 1890 and 1913; one in 1934; and another as late as 1977.[51]

People believed in Bellamy's picture of a perfect society because it was simple, logical, and appealing. Many of his contemporaries were convinced that his formula—a mixture of cooperation, brotherhood, and an industry geared to human need rather than to profit—might actually bring the utopia into being. Moreover, *Looking Backward* appealed to a public that still suffered from the effects of a deep economic depression, remained disturbed by such industrial clashes as the Haymarket riot in Chicago, and feared that other, even more spectacular crises could arise. Under these circumstances, Bellamy's humanity, ingenious plot, and confidence in humanity's inventiveness stirred elements from every class and section of the population.

After publishing *Looking Backward*, Bellamy became a propagandist for the nationalization of public services. His magazine the *Nationalist* (1889–91) helped crystallize principles that his followers wrote into the Populist platform of 1892, but although some Nationalist clubs were established, his later journal, the *New Nation,* saw the movement in decline. *Equality* (1897), a less successful sequel to *Looking Backward,* treated with prolixity problems of social organization scantily developed in his preceding novel. Two later volumes of Bellamy's uncollected writings, *Edward Bellamy Speaks Again!* (1937) and *Talks on Nationalism* (1938), seemed timely to admirers who felt that aspects of his social doctrine foreshadowed the New Deal.[52]

Bellamy's ideas found resonance in Wright's conception of democracy. In utopian Boston the machine had been fully placed at the service of humanity and of the estheticization of its life—fortuitously for Wright, Bellamy had proved Victor Hugo wrong. Bellamy's influence first appears in Wright's publications of the early 1930s, and from then on Wright often paraphrased the novelist, giving the impression that he suddenly felt enlightened. In one instance, at the Iowa County, Wisconsin, annual fair, Taliesin fellows passed out copies of chapter XXIII of *Equality* to spectators who were viewing the model of Broadacre City after it had been exhibited in New York, Madison, Pittsburgh, and Washington.[53] In that chapter, in "The Parable of the Water Tank," Bellamy addresses the ills of laissez-faire capitalism and the advantages of socialism. (While the owners of a tank become wealthy from the sale of the water and use its surplus to irrigate gardens and run decorative fountains, many of the people go thirsty. Eventually the masses take over the management of the tank in a spirit of brotherly cooperation, and all social problems are solved.)

Henry George, the nineteenth-century American economist, land reformer, and popularizer of the single tax, was another important influence on Wright's thought in this period. His *Progress and Poverty* of 1879 caught the spirit of discontent that swept the world during the great depression of 1873–78. Basing his argument on David Ricardo's doctrine of rent, he applied the laws of diminishing returns and of marginal productivity to land alone to argue that because economic progress in an industrialized society entailed a growing scarcity of land, the idle landowner reaped even greater returns at the expense of labor and capital. The proposal for which George became famous—and which Wright revived for Broadacre City—centered on the idea of taxing away all economic rent and abolishing all other taxes. (Bellamy presented this measure in *Equality* as the "tool" that bridged the "old" economic order of the nineteenth century and the new one of the year 2000. In Bellamy's scheme, by 2000 the government ran a monopoly on everything on behalf of the nation. This was one of the foundations of his utopia, since such a system would preclude all desire for lucre.) George believed, as Wright did, that the government's annual income from this single tax would be so large that there would be a surplus for public works, from roads to practically everything else.[54]

Another economic doctrine Wright favored for Broadacres was that of the Swiss economist Silvio Gesell (1862–1930). To prevent hoarding, encourage spending, and reduce interest to a minimum, Gesell proposed to make money perishable by making a banknote issued at the beginning of the year lose a fixed percentage of its face value by the end of the year.[55]

Broadacres would have never succeeded. As Norris Kelly Smith has observed, its realization "would require the abrogation of the Constitution of the United States, the elimination of thousands of government bodies from the make-up of the state, the confiscation of all lands by right of eminent domain but without compensation, the demolition of all cities and therewith the obliteration of every evidence of the country's history, the rehousing of the entire population, the retraining of millions of persons so as to enable them to be self-sustaining farmers, and other difficulties too numerous to mention. As a practicable program it does not even deserve discussion." [56] But however naïvely derived the economic and political foundations of Broadacre City may have been as a mixture of the doctrines of men like Bellamy, George, and Gesell,[57] its architecture constitutes a new departure in Wright's work and the source of what are perhaps his best buildings. This is the main value of Broadacres today, one that should be appreciated for three aspects: what it meant to Wright, what it meant to his architecture, and what it means to us.

To Wright, humankind and nature were not divided in essence. He regarded the alienation of modern humanity as simply the price we pay for having wrongly perceived civilization as a function of our own human past rather than as a product of the dictates of nature. Having come to that conclusion, he saw the great task demanded of his imagination to be the production of systems—both of architecture and of private and social behavior—that would bring human desires into closer harmony with the natural systems operating in the universe. To that end he perceived the cosmos itself as an intricate (if seemingly simple), cunningly contrived, imaginative entity. He also saw the individual as he (Wright) imagined himself to be, and thus was able to re-imagine himself as prototype. It was time to turn civilization toward integration, away from alienation, and to bring human life back into harmony with the universe.

To Wright, Broadacres was "the city that is everywhere and nowhere." To paraphrase Thomas More's pun, it was as much an *eutopia* (good place) as it was an *outopia* (no place). Wright understood that it could never be built, but he also believed that it was accessible to anyone, simply by looking into nature. Architecturally, it was a result of one of his most intense periods of artistic achievement. Through that project, to him the clearest manifestation of the Usonian idea, Wright found new purpose in his work, and he related much of his considerable remaining production to Broadacres. The Pew House was to serve as example of the "Typical Home for Sloping Ground"; St. Mark's Tower (later the Price Company Tower, Bartlesville, Oklahoma) was to be the "Typical Accommodation for the City-Dweller as yet Unlearned Where Ground is Concerned"; the "Monumental Pole Announcing Festivals" by the County Fairgrounds eventually became the Illinois Tower project; the Marin County Courthouse also found its source in a building of Broadacres; and the list of examples could grow longer. More important, his conception of the Usonian House, an idea that revolutionized American residential architecture, also had its source in Broadacres. This explains why Wright paid so much attention to the First Jacobs House; it was the first Usonian structure he built.

On another level, Broadacres remains significant as a metaphor that illuminates the depth and breadth of Wright's architectural vision. It synthesizes his ideals for us. In Broadacres he made the machine the basis of the new world, an ambition he had enunciated at the turn of the century in "The Art and Craft of the Machine." In that address he had argued that Victor Hugo had been correct in his assumptions but wrong in his conclusions, an idea Wright carried through his Usonian period.

Two results of Wright's interest in mechanization were the

Usonian method of construction, a combination of wood sandwich wall and brick, and the Usonian Automatic, a system based on concrete blocks. Ostensibly this was prefabrication at the service of the democratic individual, and for two purposes. One was to ease labor, and the other was to express openly in the design of modest middle-class dwellings the rhythms and messages that sages of long ago had concealed in the *hermetica*, and had expressed only in cathedrals and other buildings of high function. In Wright's new democratic world all buildings would be equally noble because their importance would be grounded in designs based on nature, not on false hierarchies of functions conceived by humankind.

In Broadacres Wright also gave substance to Viollet-le-Duc's dream of a style that would be as efficient as nature's at creating character, and he extended that style beyond buildings to redesign a nation. This he offered to ordinary men and women not only as a basis for a new architecture, as he had during the Prairie period, but as the cornerstone of the utopia. The intensity of that idea and the enthusiasm that it generated in Wright thrust him into searching for an entirely new conception of architecture. Three characteristics of his work are more evident in this period than in any other: an extraordinary mastery of planning and structure, the use of compositional rhythms with musical undertones, and the expression of the Taoist concept of the fundamental existentiality of vacuity. The result was the Usonian House, "Fallingwater," the Johnson Wax Building, Taliesin West, and the Guggenheim Museum.

Broadacres is the most complete architectural expression of the American jeremiad. No architectural dream has been more comprehensive in its desire to turn its back on history and embrace the American ideal of covenant (except, perhaps, for Amish communities). Usonia would have comprised something similar to thousands of Amish communities that somehow had become secularized, electrified, and mechanized, that had substituted nature for Jehovah, and that had traded a religious ideal for an esthetic one. "Eventually we must live for the Beautiful, whether we want to or not," Wright had said in one of his Princeton lectures.[58] Groupings of enlightened gentleman farmers would supplant the *civitas* as the basis of civilization. Democracy, in Wright's understanding, was "an innate aristocracy,"[59] an idea that may well have come from his Lloyd-Jones family through his mother, and one with which his third wife agreed wholeheartedly. Apprentices at Taliesin were asked to share in household chores because in her opinion "hired help *vulgarized* the Fellowship."[60]

That was an opinion consistent with the jeremiad-like character of the Fellowship, as Mrs. Wright—echoing Gurdjieff—understood it (but not perhaps her husband, for whom the Fellowship was a more down-to-earth institution). In the context of Mrs. Wright's thought, the jeremiad implied a ritualizing of everyday behavior. Such was the nature of its sacramental character. That sacramental character, in turn, related to archetypes established by nature, perhaps at the all-important and magical moment when chaos became cosmos. Humanity was to fulfill its destiny by returning to that perfect, mythical, and extra-temporal moment before the first crotchet of history had taken place. Such was the mandate of nature.

Wright, on the other hand, always related the Fellowship to his architecture, which he had always seen as part of a larger scheme for the estheticization of life. Ideals he had espoused in his Prairie period through William Gannett's *The House Beautiful*—which at the time he could no more than suggest to his clients—were now to be enforced in Broadacres, and by extension at Taliesin. His apprentices, for example, were asked to submit the designs for their own private rooms to his approval.[61] Similarly, the highest official in Broadacre City was to be the County Architect, who, although popularly elected, would have almost supreme powers to regulate the appearance of the community, down to the details of private dwellings, in order to ensure a continuity of organic conception in all aspects of design.

Broadacres is also a paradox. In it Wright brought together nineteenth-century ideals of communion with nature, of the brotherhood of humankind, and of a style based on nature. With these he created an architecture universally described as representing an advanced twentieth-century style. In the end, however, the paradox is irrelevant. Wright's importance lies neither in the intellectual sphere nor in the field of social ideas, but in the realm of tangible architecture. His covenant, from beginning to end, was not established directly with nature, but with the beauty that nature extended to humanity—to Wright himself, if not to any other—for him to enjoy and emulate.

## NOTES

1. Wright's most important publications on this subject are: *Modern Architecture: Being the Kahn Lectures for 1930 by Frank Lloyd Wright* (Princeton: Princeton University Press, 1931; reprint, Carbondale: Southern Illinois University Press, 1987); *The Disappearing City* (New York: William Farquhar Payson, 1932); "Broadacre City: A New Community Plan," *Architectural Record*, 77 (April 1935), pp. 243–254; "The New Frontier: Broadacre City," *Taliesin Fellowship Publications* 1 (October 1940); *When Democracy Builds* (Chicago: University of Chicago Press, 1945); *The Living City* (New York: Horizon, 1958); and *The Industrial Revolution Runs Away* (New York: Horizon, 1969). For these and other bibliographical entries on the subject, see under "Broadacre City (project)," in the index of Robert L. Sweeney, *Frank Lloyd Wright: An Annotated Bibliography* (Los Angeles: Hennessey and Ingalls, 1978).

2. Norris Kelly Smith, *Frank Lloyd Wright: A Study in Arhictectural Content* (New York: Prentice-Hall, 1966), pp. 157–168, touched on some characteristics of Wright's thought that link him to the jeremiad, but failed to make a direct connection.

3. Sacvan Bercovitch, *The American Jeremiad* (Madison: University of Wisconsin Press, 1978), p. xv.

4. David W. Noble, *Historians against History: The Frontier Thesis and the National Covenant in American Historical Writing since 1830* (Minneapolis: University of Minnesota Press, 1965), p. 3.

5. Bercovitch, p. 164.

6. Some sources where these themes are discussed are Henry Nash Smith, *Virgin Land: The American West as Symbol and Myth* (Cambridge: Harvard University Press, 1950); Richard Warrington Lewis, *The American Adam: Innocence, Tragedy and Tradition in the Nineteenth Century* (Chicago: University of Chicago Press, 1953); David Watson Noble, *The Eternal Adam and the New World Garden: The Central Myth in the American Novel since 1830* (New York: Braziller, 1968); and Merle Curti, *Human Nature in American Thought: A History* (Madison: University of Wisconsin Press, 1980).

7. Jeremiah 31: 33–34.

8. Quotations from Whitman's "Democratic Vistas," in Floyd Stoval, ed., *Walt Whitman: Representative Selections* (1934; New York: Hill and Wang, 1961), pp. 434, 391, 389, 410, 390, 405.

9. *Ibid.*, p. 379.

10. *Ibid.*

11. Maginel Wright Barney, *The Valley of the God-Almighty Joneses* (New York: Appleton-Century, 1965), p. 60.

12. Victor Hugo, *Notre-Dame de Paris*, 2 vols. (New York: Booklover Press, n.d.), I, p. 214.

13. *Ibid.*, pp. 205–206 (conversation between Frollo and Louis XI).

14. *Ibid.*, p. 220.

15. *Ibid.*, p. 224.

16. Frank Lloyd Wright, preface to *Ausgeführte Bauten und Entwürfe von Frank Lloyd Wright* (Berlin: Wasmuth, 1910), unpaged.

17. Wright, "The Art and Craft of the Machine," in Edgar Kaufmann and Ben Raeburn, eds., *Frank Lloyd Wright: Writings and Buildings* (1960; New York: Meridian, 1970), p. 67.

18. Donald Hoffmann, "Frank Lloyd Wright and Viollet-le-Duc," *Journal of the Society of Architectural Historians*, 28 (October 1969), pp. 173–183, points out that Wright began reading Viollet-le-Duc in Madison, and that in spite of his assertions to the contrary in *An Autobiography* (New York: Duell, Sloan and Pearce, 1943), pp. 53, 75, he did not read the *Dictionnaire raisonné*—since he had no French—but only the *Discourses*, possibly in the Van Brunt translation, and *The Habitation of Man in All Ages*.

19. Eugène Viollet-le-Duc, "Style," *Dictionnaire raisonné de l'architecture française du XIe au XVIe siècle* (Paris: Morel, 1854–69), VIII, p. 475.

20. Viollet-le-Duc, *Discourses on Architecture,* translated by Henry Van Brunt (Boston: James R. Osgood, 1875), p. 179.

21. Besides paraphrasing Viollet-le-Duc's passage in *Ausgeführte Bauten,* Wright also stated these ideas in his introduction to the catalogue of Japanese prints in the Art Institute of Chicago, 1906, in Frederick Gutheim, ed., *Frank Lloyd Wright on Architecture: Selected Writings (1894–1940)* (New York: Grosset and Dunlap, 1941), p. 122; and in *The Japanese Print: An Interpretation* (1912; New York: Horizon, 1967), p. 14.

22. Viollet-le-Duc, "Style," p. 480.

23. *Ibid.,* pp. 482–485.

24. Viollet-le-Duc, "Proportion," *Dictionnaire,* VII, pp. 532–561; *Discourses,* p. 433.

25. Wright, *An Autobiography,* p. 423.

26. *Ibid.,* p. 225.

27. *Ibid.,* p. 422.

28. Wright, *An Autobiography* (London: Faber and Faber, 1946), p. 201; quoted by Leonard Eaton, *Two Chicago Architects and Their Clients: Frank Lloyd Wright and Howard Van Doren Shaw* (Cambridge: MIT Press, 1969), p. 46. This passage appears in no other edition of the *Autobiography.*

29. Wright, *An Autobiography* (1943), p. 227.

30. Eaton, pp. 46–49.

31. Wright, *Ausgeführte Bauten,* unpaged.

32. Wright, "In the Cause of Architecture," *Architectural Record,* 63 (January 1928), pp. 49–57.

33. Wright, "Principles of Design," *Annual of American Design* (1931), pp. 101–104; this quotation, p. 101.

34. *Ibid.,* p. 101.

35. Wright,, *An Autobiography,* p. 420.

36. For a wider discussion of these aspects, see Narciso G. Menocal, "Frank Lloyd Wright and the Question of Style," *Journal of Decorative and Propaganda Arts,* 2 (Summer/Fall 1986), pp. 4–19.

37. For a discussion of some of these projects, see Robert C. Twombly, *Frank Lloyd Wright: His Life and His Architecture* (New York: John Wiley and Sons, 1979), pp. 223–227.

38. The facts of her life are well known. Born in 1898 as Olga Milanoff, daughter of a Montenegrin supreme court justice, she was educated in Czarist Russia and in Turkey. While still in her teens, she married the architect Vlademar Hinzenberg, and in 1917 gave him a daughter, Svetlana. From 1920 to 1924 she was first a pupil and then an instructor in Georgi Gurdjieff's Institute for the Harmonious Development of Man in Fontainebleau. She met Wright on November 30, 1924, at a performance of the Petrograd Ballet in Chicago; by February she was living in Taliesin. She married Wright on August 25, 1928. She died on March 2, 1985.

39. For these events, see Wright, *An Autobiography,* pp. 301–560. See also Twombly, pp. 192–236.

40. Richard Jones, Wright's grandfather, had arrived in Wisconsin in 1846, some two years after landing in New York from Wales on December 8, 1844. By the spring of 1856 he had bought land by the Wisconsin River. The valley did not become Jones property until 1865 or 1866. See Barney, *The Valley of the God-Almighty Joneses,* pp. 36, 45–46, 49.

41. Wright, *An Autobiography,* pp. 5–9.

42. Twombly, pp. 211–212.

43. Wright, *Modern Architecture,* pp. 41–42.

44. *Ibid.,* pp. 393–394.

45. *Ibid.,* p. 402.

46. Sterling Sorensen, "Wright's Taliesin is League of Nations in Miniature," *Capital Times* (Madison, Wisconsin), September 28, 1947. Quoted in Twombly, "Organic Living: Frank Lloyd Wright's Taliesin Fellowship and Georgi Gurdjieff's Institute for the Harmonious Development of Man," *Wisconsin Magazine of History,* 58 (Winter 1974–75), pp. 126–139; this quotation, p. 132.

47. Quoted in Twombly, "Organic Living," p. 137.

48. Smith, p. 148.

49. Robert Fishman, *Urban Utopias in the Twentieth Century: Ebenezer Howard, Frank Lloyd Wright, and Le Corbusier* (Cambridge: MIT Press, 1982), p. 33.

50. Arthur O. Lewis, *Utopian Literature in The Pennsylvania State University Libraries: A Selected Bibliography* (University Park: The Pennsylvania State University Libraries, 1984), p. 11.

51. Scanning through Lewis, one finds the following titles: Arthur Bird, *Looking Forward: A Dream of the United States of the Americas in 1999* (Utica, N.Y.: Press of L. C. Childs and Sons, 1899); Paul Devinne, *The Day of Prosperity: A Vision of the Century to Come* (New York: G. W. Dillingham Company, 1902); Ignatius Donnelly, *Caesar's Column: A Story of the Twentieth Century* (Chicago: F. J. Schulte and Company, 1890); Alvarado Mortimer Fuller, *A.D. 2000: A Novel* (Chicago: Laird and Lee, 1890); Ludwig A. Geissler, *Looking Beyond: A Sequel to "Looking Backward," by Edward Bellamy, and an Answer to "Looking Further Forward," by Richard Michaelis* (London: William Reeves, 1891); Harry W. Hillman, *Looking Forward: The Phenomenal Progress of Electricity in 1912* (Northampton, Mass.: Valley View Publishing Company, 1906); Albert Adams Merrill, *The Great Awakening: The Story of the Twenty-Second Century* (Boston: George Book Publishing Co., 1899); Richard C. Michaelis, *Looking Further Forward: An Answer to Looking Backward by Edward Bellamy* (Chicago and New York: Rand, McNally, 1890); William Morris, *News from Nowhere, or An Epoch of Rest, Being Some Chapters from a Utopian Romance* (Boston: Roberts Brothers, 1890; London: Reeves and Turner, 1891); Hugh Pedley, *Looking Forward: The Strange Experience of the Reverend Fergus McCheyne* (Toronto: William Briggs, 1913); Mack Reynolds, *Equality: In the Year 2000* (New York: Ace Books, 1977); J. W. Roberts, *Looking Within: The Misleading Tendencies of*

"*Looking Backward*" *Made Manifest* (New York: A. S. Barnes and Company, 1893); W. W. Satterlee, *Looking Backward: And What I Saw 1890–2101* (Minneapolis: Harrison and Smith, 1890); Solomon Schindler, *Young West: A Sequel to Edward Bellamy's Celebrated Novel "Looking Backward"* (Boston: Arena Publishing Company, 1894); Arthur Dudley Vinton, *Looking Further Backward* (Albany, N.Y.: Albany Book Company, 1890); Conrad Wilbrandt, *Des Herrn Friedrich Ost Erlebnisse in der Welt Bellamys: Mittelungen aus den Jahren 2001 und 2002* (Weimar, 1891); and Cuthbert Yerex, *Christopher Brand: Looking Forward* (Los Angeles: Wetzel Publishing Company, 1934).

52. For Bellamy, see Arthur E. Morgan, *Edward Bellamy* (New York: Columbia University Press, 1944); Sylvia E. Bowman, *The Year 2000: A Critical Biography of Edward Bellamy* (New York: Bookman Associates, 1958); Daniel Aaron, *Men of Good Hope: A Story of American Progressives* (New York: Oxford University Press, 1961); John L. Thomas, "Utopia for an Urban Age: Henry George, Henry Demarest Lloyd, Edward Bellamy," *Perspectives in American History*, 2 (1972), pp. 135–163; and T. M. Parsinnen, "Bellamy, Morris, and the Image of the Industrial City in Victorian Social Criticism," *Midwest Quarterly*, 14 (April 1973), pp. 257–266.

53. "A Note on the Models," *Taliesin*, 1 (October 1940); *The New Frontier: Broadacre City*, p. 24.

54. For Henry George, see Steven B. Cord, *Henry George: Dreamer or Realist?* (Philadelphia: University of Pennsylvania Press, 1965); Anna George DeMille, *Henry George*, ed. by D. C. Shoemaker (Chapel Hill: University of North Carolina Press, 1950); and Charles Albro Barker, *Henry George: Citizen of the World* (New York: Oxford University Press, 1955).

55. For Gesell, see Willy Hess, *Die Werke von Silvio Gesell* (Bern: Verlag Freiwirtschaftlicher Schriften, 1975).

56. Smith, pp. 153–154.

57. The model of Broadacres carries an inscription on two columns. The first column reads: "Broadacres commemorates: Moses, Spartacus, Heraclitus, Goethe, Mazzini, Count Tolstoi, Prince Peter Kropotkin, Silvo [*sic*] Gesell, Henry Thoreau, William Blake, Louis Sullivan. Not forgetting: F. L. Wright [added], Thorsten [*sic*] Veblen, Edward Bellamy." The second column carries the following: "Required reading for students of Broadacre [*sic*]: Laotze, Jesus, Spinoza, Voltaire, Walt Whitman, Henry George, William Blake, Louis Sullivan, F. L. WRIGHT [added]. Not forgetting: Nietzsche, Thoreau, Emerson."

58. Wright, *Modern Architecture*, p. 113.

59. Wright, *An Autobiography*, p. 455.

60. *Ibid.*, p. 424.

61. *Ibid.*, p. 426.

# ⊡. THE SECOND CAREER: 1924–1959
*Bruce Brooks Pfeiffer*

Had he designed and built nothing else after 1924, Frank Lloyd Wright would still rank as one of the greatest architects in history. Alone and unaided, he had created organic architecture, that profound and yet simple concept that buildings must develop naturally out of their environment, reflect their central purpose, and use the building materials best suited to those two factors.

Organic architecture gave life to the Prairie houses flowing low and long across the level Midwestern plains. It led to pioneer structure and form in milestone buildings such as the Larkin Building and Unity Temple, self-contained monoliths that maximized the ideas of fluid interior space and also gave rise to the International Style. Breeding grounds for innovation, the Larkin introduced air-conditioning, plate glass doors, metal furniture, and a host of other firsts, while Unity Temple made the first important use of poured concrete in architecture.

Chicago's Midway Gardens, with its incredible profusion of design, was behind him, as was the Imperial Hotel in Tokyo, a

breakthrough engineering statement as well as an architectural one. By the early 1920s Frank Lloyd Wright had developed the concrete block system, which he called "textile block," and his four houses in the Los Angeles area built on that system stand today as four remarkable achievements. Finally in 1924 he designed the National Life Insurance skyscraper for Chicago. A great structure of reinforced concrete, sheet metal, and glass, it was to be the quintessence of the tall building, a prophet of all the towering American skyscrapers to come.

With all these achievements to his name as he approached the age of 60, it would seem that Frank Lloyd Wright's career had reached its apogee. Dione Neutra, the wife of the architect Richard Neutra, visited Mr. Wright in 1924 and was struck by how passive and isolated he seemed. To her, all that talent and genius lay almost fallow while lesser architects across the country garnered lucrative commissions. Added to the factor of age and isolation were the scandals, terrible in those days, of divorce and adultery. No wonder Mrs. Neutra and other European visitors viewed him then as a legendary figure out of the past.

Yet in his sixties, seventies, and eighties, right up to the age of 92—his "majority," as he described those last three decades of his life—Frank Lloyd Wright would experience a burst of

Bruce Brooks Pfeiffer studied at the Taliesin Fellowship (1949–56) and at the Ecole Supéricure des Beaux-Arts, Paris (1956–57). He is Director of Archives for the Frank Lloyd Wright Foundation. His publications include exhibition catalogs, architectural guides, texts for a series of Japanese monographs on Wright's architecture, and four books of letters from Frank Lloyd Wright to his apprentices, architects, clients, and others, most recently *The Guggenheim Correspondence* (1986).

creativity unprecedented in the annals of architecture. The result would be a flowering of ideas, of forms, of shapes, of innovations staggering to behold, an outpouring whose volume increased from one year to the next. Most of his "famous" works would be products of these years, along with the legend that surrounded him then and even now.

It would be easy to dismiss his renaissance of creativity as something unaccountable, the inexplicable product of old age, like the late great plays of Sophocles or the ultimate sculpted visions of Michelangelo hardly risen from the stone. One might stand and marvel at such works as "miracles" out of the vacuum of old age. But in truth all such miracles are complex products inevitably rooted in living. And those remarkable products, in the case of Frank Lloyd Wright, can be traced to two factors, different in circumstance yet essentially intertwined to form a unified whole. One was his marriage to Olga Ivanovna Lazovich Hinzenberg; the other was his founding of the Taliesin Fellowship, through whose offices many young men and women were given an architectural education unique in history.

Frank Lloyd Wright and Olgivanna, as he learned to call her, met at a ballet concert in Chicago in the autumn of 1924. He was almost 60, with gray hair receding at the temples. She was in her twenties, demure and regal, of exceptional beauty. The attraction was instantaneous, despite the fact that neither of them was free. He, the father of six children, was seeking a divorce from his second wife. She, the mother of a seven-year-old daughter, was also seeking a divorce. "Come with me, Olgivanna," he told her on that first afternoon, "and they will not see us for the dust!" She did, and when the litigious dust was settled they married at Rancho Santa Fe, California, in 1928.

Olgivanna, the daughter of a Montenegrin judge, was broadly educated in the liberal arts. She had been a student and disciple of G. I. Gurdjieff, a mystic whose path to self-understanding was by way of rigorous self-discipline. She studied under Gurdjieff for seven years, in Russia, Paris, and Fontainebleau, before coming to the United States in the wake of the Russian Revolution. "For more than 30 years," wrote one biographer, "she would remain devotedly at Wright's side, fortifying him with the kind of warm sympathy and inspiration that men of genius need if they are to keep on creating. . . . Much of his later achievement was made directly possible by the contentment and happiness that she brought to his life."

On the surface, at least, Frank Lloyd Wright's marriage to the lovely and gifted young woman was ideal. And that idealism was reflected in the work he began at this time, notably the plans for San Marcos-in-the-Desert drawn up in 1928. The client was Dr. Alexander Chandler, a veterinarian who had founded the town of Chandler, some twenty miles southeast of Phoenix. The project was to be an immense hotel complex skirting the South Mountain Range outside of Chandler. Each room was to have its own sunny terrace, plunge pool, and terrace-garden. Not only the rooms but also all the corridors, closets, bathrooms, and storage areas were to be top-lit. Sunlight would pour in everywhere. The San Marcos concept was practical—Mr. Wright never designed anything that could not be built—but the stock market crash of 1929 wiped out most of the financiers from New York who, along with Dr. Chandler himself, were backing the project. Ultimately plans for the hotel were abandoned and it is perhaps just as well, since building San Marcos as an adjunct to the unlikely town of Chandler would be like putting a gold crown on the head of

a peasant. It belonged more suitably on the rocky slopes of Montenegro.

As early as 1928 Frank Lloyd Wright made plans for a school in Wisconsin, to be called the Hillside Home School for the Allied Arts, using the Hillside Home School buildings that he had designed in 1886 and 1902. This 1928 scheme as proposed proved too ambitious, and the project was abandoned. But in 1932 Mr. and Mrs. Wright, using their own home, Taliesin, as a base of operations, succeeded in founding a very special kind of school. Guest rooms were converted into apprentice rooms, the kitchen and dining room on the hill above Taliesin's living quarters were made larger, and other spaces and rooms were expanded or altered to accommodate the 32 persons who came on opening day, October 23. Drafting boards and stools were added in the studio, and the old farm buildings at Hillside, a quarter of a mile away, were made ready for a fully functioning farm, complete with dairy herd, beef cattle, chickens, hogs, and sheep.

Both Wrights had become convinced through early training that learning by doing was an educational must. And for both of them "doing" meant bedrock practical chores as well as technical and artistic training. As a small boy Frank Lloyd Wright had been sent by his mother to work each summer at his uncle's farm in the ancestral Lloyd-Jones valley in Wisconsin. This early training he considered a strong contributing factor to his subsequent growth and development. For her part, Olgivanna in her years at the Gurdjieff Institute had received intensive training in housework, gardening, cooking, and building construction, along with music, rhythmic dance, ethics, and philosophy. Quite naturally, therefore, the architectural training of the Taliesin Fellowship would range from cattle raising to design, from dishwashing to creativity. "We must have our feet firm on the ground, and then we can consort with the stars," Mr. Wright explained to the Fellowship.

Three main phases made up the work of the Fellowship: work in the studio, work on construction, and work on maintenance. The apprentices would learn the craft of architecture by participating in the architectural work of Frank Lloyd Wright. They would learn building construction by actual work on buildings: stonemasonry, carpentry, wiring, plumbing, landscaping, interior design, furniture-making, and eventually weaving, pottery, and sculpture. Finally, maintenance work in all its phases would be shared by all, from kitchen work, cleaning, decorating, and repairing to the field work on the farm.

At the outset, with few or no commissions coming in, Frank Lloyd Wright devoted himself and his apprentices to a project new in kind to him and vaster in scope than any he had previously undertaken: Broadacre City. It was designed to be an archetypal model of the new American city, four square miles in size, an ideal community. He described it in the *Architectural Record* as containing "little farms, little homes for industry, little factories, little schools, a little university going to the people." Its aim was to end the unemployment of the Great Depression of the 1930s, and for the young apprentices working on the Broadacre City model in Chandler, Arizona, in 1934 it seemed a dream come true. Frank Lloyd Wright must surely have known, however, how youthfully visionary this project was. The stern realities of the Great Depression had people flocking to the big cities instead of away from them. At least in the cities there were some jobs to be found, and Hoovervilles, and at worst soup kitchens. The decentralized world that Broadacre City envisioned was as much an ideal as San Marcos-in-the-Desert.

Nevertheless both projects exhibited a scope and expansiveness that signaled the great surge of creativity to come. The ideal that illuminated them both reflected the educational ideal of the Taliesin Fellowship as well as the ideal marriage wherein Olgivanna brought "contentment and happiness" to the life of Frank Lloyd Wright.

To ascribe the creative outburst of 1935–59 simply to idealism, however, would be to mistake the part for the whole. There was also tumult and tension, and agony as well as joy. And if we search more deeply for the causes, we find all of the motive forces in the marriage and the Taliesin Fellowship along with the idealism.

An incident early in their life together offers a complicating angle of vision. Shortly after their first meeting, Olgivanna invited Lisa, a European friend, to Wisconsin for the weekend. Mr. Wright arranged an outing for the three of them on the lake below Taliesin, a candle-lit evening supper on shipboard. It was to be a charming, romantic occasion, except that the mosquitoes were out in hordes. For some reason mosquitoes never attacked Mr. Wright, but the ladies were tormented by them, and Olgivanna implored him to turn around and go back to the shore. He would not. Though both women were sobbing and pleading with him, he angrily replied that he had gone to a great deal of hard work to prepare the boat with its decorations and candles and he would not turn back.

Two years later, when they were living near Chandler and working on the plans for San Marcos-in-the-Desert, Olgivanna purchased a brightly colored silk dress that underscored her youthful beauty. Mr. Wright resented that dress intensely, often

told her so, and finally went to her closet, removed it, and stuffed it into a trash container.

Although these and similar early incidents were individually of little moment, they did reveal that the marriage was made on earth and subject to an inevitable human predicament. Married to a woman 32 years his junior, Frank Lloyd Wright was troubled in those first years by the conflict between youth and age. As he felt himself moving into life's final phase, he was aware that Olgivanna's life was just beginning. Youth against age, life against death: these conflicts, buried deep, would have profound effects on his life and work. Despite the love and harmony genuinely there, they would flare up at times in shows of petty cruelty, as resentment of youth, and as a new emotion in his life: jealousy.

Among those he was jealous of early on were the sculptor Carl Milles and the architect Eero Saarinen. He was even jealous of his wife's writing, with the result that Olgivanna, a gifted author in her own right, was obliged to conceal her efforts from her husband until the very last years of his life. "Your jealousy, Frank," she once confronted him, "is of such a cosmic nature that if you were to subscribe to the idea of reincarnation you would have to come back many times to overcome it."

In a similar vein the Taliesin Fellowship, with its educational ideals and host of loyal and dedicated students, offered its own conflicts between youth and age, life and death. The apprentices' lives, like Olgivanna's, seemed to Mr. Wright to be just beginning while his was moving into history. And Frank Lloyd Wright soon learned that, no matter how devoted to him they were, most of them moved on in a year or two. In a sense he was continually saying goodbye to youth and affection. Some students, moreover, disliked the strict regimen and left abruptly, "taking a pot of coals," as Mr. Wright put it, "and going out and starting a little hell of their own." More telling was his frequent admonition: "As long as you're an inspiration to me, I'll be one to you. When you cease to be one to me you will find that you don't like it here—that this isn't what you thought it was."

Spurred by this mixture of new-found youth and encroaching age, of life at once ascending and descending, of having and not yet holding, the masterpieces of the 1930s and early 1940s appeared. First "Fallingwater," for Edgar Kaufmann, at Mill Run, Pennsylvania, followed the next year by the Johnson Wax Building at Racine, Wisconsin, and the masterpiece home for Herbert Johnson himself, "Wingspread." At the same time Frank Lloyd Wright developed a new building system, the Usonian House, for Herbert Jacobs, near Madison, Wisconsin, wherein he proved that the average American citizen of moderate means could live in a beautiful home appropriate to a democracy. The Jacobs House as prototype was followed by a large number of Usonian homes across the nation.

The 1930s also produced the Hanna House, in Stanford, California, Mr. Wright's first experiment in the hexagon plan and unit system. The Jester House for Palos Verdes, California, presented his first all-circular plan for residential living. The innovative campus for Florida Southern College—innovative in the sense of being a design suited to the Florida region rather than a conglomerate of European styles—fell into those years, as did the spectacular Monona Terrace Civic Center for Madison, Wisconsin, and the Crystal Heights Hotel and Towers for Washington, D.C. A housing project for Los Angeles, the All-Steel Houses, saw the invention of yet another building system.

By 1944 Frank Lloyd Wright and his Taliesin Fellowship

had turned out 152 new buildings and projects. If there was any constant during this period, it was change: change in the expected appearance of things, as in "Fallingwater" and the Johnson Administration Building; change in materials, from steel to desert rock to pressed earth; change in basic shape, from square to hexagon to circle. And those changes were mirrored in the life around him, at home with Olgivanna, and in the drafting that he did with the Fellowship.

For Olgivanna it began in 1935 with the arrival of a new apprentice, Cornelia (Kay) Schneider, from Switzerland. Until that time Olgivanna, a near-contemporary of the apprentices, was considered more their peer than their mentor, although she and Mr. Wright were co-founders of the school. Kay, however, was barely fifteen, young enough to gravitate to Mrs. Wright for guidance and counsel. During the next several years other young apprentices arrived who along with Kay formed a nucleus of people impressed by Mrs. Wright's knowledge of philosophy and human nature. They found that they could learn from her as well as from Mr. Wright, and she in turn made it possible for them to gain closer contact with her architect husband. She had gone from a young, beautiful woman in her twenties to a mature woman with a deepened sense of wisdom and human ethics. Her hair was now gray, with two streaks artfully streaming from the temples in a style all her own. Her dignity and age, and with it a more profound type of beauty, brought her closer now to the stature of Mr. Wright: they walked together as a well-matched couple, not as an older man with his young bride. There were still conflicts with disenchanted youth in the Fellowship, and with Olgivanna flare-ups, small hurts, even bouts of jealousy. But all of these, to quote Mrs. Wright, had grown less "cosmic."

For him the struggle and tension, the bitterness and anger and hurt, had lessened. He had learned to feed upon her vital youthfulness, to accept it, to be comfortable with it, and in many ways he now seemed to grow younger as he grew older. "Many of the buds of the stem at sixteen are in blossom now," he wrote at that time; "'young' is only a circumstance while 'youth' is a quality."

Paralleling this change in their relations came a change in the Fellowship. Mr. Wright's "boys and girls," as he called us, still arrived and left, and there were still dissenters. But there were converts, too, young men and women who like Kay stayed on to become what Mr. Wright described as "the fingers on my hand."

After 1935, as the work picked up, those who remained longer were assigned a new role: supervising the construction of the various new buildings. Apprentice Robert Mosher went to "Fallingwater"; Edgar Tafel to the Johnson Buildings; Kenn Lockhart to the Florida Southern campus in Lakeland.

Some did even more. Like Mrs. Wright they served as full partners in aspects of his work. Conspicuous among them were William Wesley Peters, John Howe, and Eugene Masselink.

Wes Peters, second only to Mr. Wright in his knowledge of building construction, was sent everywhere when an emergency arose, and for more extreme problems and difficulties he accompanied Mr. Wright himself. Trained as an engineer, Wes could see the genius of Mr. Wright's constantly new innovations in structure and then find ways of making them intelligible to the world of engineers. It was he who helped to figure out the formulas for such structures as the Johnson Administration Building with its dendriform columns, the Guggenheim Museum with its continuously expanding spiral, the Johnson Research Tower with its taproot foundation and cantilevered floor slabs, the Kansas City Community Church,

the Pittsburgh Point Civic Center projects, and later on the Unitarian Church in Madison, the Price Tower in Bartlesville, Oklahoma, and many more—the list is practically endless.

John Howe arrived at Taliesin as a boy of eighteen with no college training. But he possessed a gift for drawing that was nothing short of astonishing. Any sketch of Mr. Wright's placed before Jack would soon be interpreted into a final perspective. Mr. Wright could then return to the drafting board and render the perspective—i.e., put in color, shading, and vibrant touches as only he could do. To watch the two of them work together was to witness a magic metamorphosis occurring on a sheet of paper.

Eugene Masselink was an artist studying at the University of Michigan in 1932 when he arranged for Frank Lloyd Wright to come and deliver a lecture at Ann Arbor. Soon after, he became a Taliesin Fellow. Besides serving as Mr. Wright's secretary, business manager, and general factotum, Gene had a natural talent for abstract design. Working at Taliesin he became totally immersed in the geometric, unit-system style employed by Mr. Wright in such designs as the stained glass of the earlier years, the rugs for the Imperial Hotel, and the murals for both the Hotel and Midway Gardens.

Instinctively attracted to this kind of work and quick to absorb its underlying idea, Gene went on to develop his own style and character, at which point Mr. Wright turned over to him all subsequent graphic and abstract layouts. Murals and screens for dozens of clients were designed and executed by Gene, including the Price Tower mural, the screen for the Thomas Keys House in Rochester, Minnesota, and the icons for the Greek Orthodox Church in Wauwatosa, Wisconsin.

By 1950 even the apprentices who left were not entirely gone. Many of them became extensions of Mr. Wright's work in various cities and countries: Aaron Green in San Francisco, Kelly Oliver in Denver, Raku Endo in Tokyo, Nezam Ameri in Teheran, Morton Delson in New York, Marya Lilien in Chicago, and Mr. Wright's own grandson Eric in Los Angeles.

As a result of all this activity, the decade from 1944 to 1954 was even more productive than any that had preceded it. The ceaseless creative force and artistic energy of Frank Lloyd Wright fed into every avenue of architecture and engineering.

With the design of two particular structures, the Guggenheim Museum and the Johnson Research Tower, a new grammar of form began to emerge. More curvilinear, more fluid, more plastic in shape and form, these buildings showed an exuberant sense of geometry almost lyric in character. The studio residence for Franklin Watkins in Barnegat City, New Jersey, offered this same geometric lyricism in wood construction, as did the studio for Arch Oboler in Malibu, California, and the summer house for John Stamm on Lake Delavan, Wisconsin. A similar lyricism informed the designs for the Pittsburgh Point Twin Bridges, to be built out of reinforced concrete and steel cables—what he called "the spider spinning." The gentle softness of the curved line was a permanent feature of his work from this point onward. The Haldorn House on the coast at Carmel, California, is, as its name "The Wave" implies, a concrete, glass, and steel abstraction of the ceaseless movement of water. The large spiral Civic Center for Pittsburgh is another, far larger application of the ramp theme used in the Guggenheim Museum. The V. C. Morris Shop in San Francisco takes a common city lot space, square and uninteresting, and remodels it into a gracious space of everflowing lines.

In his last five years the work of Frank Lloyd Wright took on yet another dimension. A great simplicity emerged, a simplicity that evokes a spiritual quality. The space within the Beth Sholom Synagogue in Elkins Park, Pennsylvania, is exalted, permeated with a sense of humanity and divinity united as one. The design for the Christian Science Church in Bolinas, California, reflects this same amalgam. Of this project Frank Lloyd Wright wrote: "Temple of the Mind—the Mind taking precedence over the Spirit—Intelligence above feeling, putting Mind above Spirit by calling Spirit Mind."

The Greek Orthodox Church is a simple cross in plan, rising to support a disk. The little shop-kiosks he designed for Baghdad are elemental cubes supporting offset spheres—the cube on the ground for sales, the sphere riding over it for storage. The Marin County Civic Center in California is but a simple bridge of three levels connecting the existing hills. Large arches support the building; smaller arches on the upper levels hang pendant-like from the slab edges to form sun-shields. After six sets of working drawings, the Guggenheim Museum, as built from the 1956 drawings, possesses a far greater simplicity than the design of 1943. In the last years of his work, the fluidity that emerged in 1943 has blended with and become transcended by a type of pure geometry. He now has become full master of his art; his sketches are minimal because the idea is perfectly clear right from the very inception of each project.

During those last five years it seemed that every year, indeed every month, saw the creation of newer forms, newer spaces, newer techniques of building and construction. More important, however, each new work saw Mr. Wright's own deeper and deeper understanding of organic architecture as the "Thing in Itself." By 1957 he could state in his TV interview with Mike Wallace: "Now I can just shake the designs out of my sleeve."

In 1928 Mr. Wright's early client W. E. Martin's response to his third marriage was "I hope this is your last, since you have already gone through two other marriages." Mr. Wright's reply was simple: "No, not my last, but my first; the others were merely dress rehearsals!"

Now time had turned those brave words into truth. His life with Olgivanna had become everything romantics saw it as from the beginning. The unease was gone, and the tension, and the jealousy. When she published her book *Our House* in 1958 he was delighted by her achievement. And when she brought him the first copy he was especially delighted by the dedication: "Dedicated to Frank Lloyd Wright himself." It seemed to form some sort of perfect circle in relation to a dedication he had written to her in his own book *An Autobiography*: "To my co-author Olgivanna from her own 'author'—Frank Lloyd Wright."

When they first met she knew little of architecture but had a profound sense of human aspirations and potential. From the very beginning, a mutual exchange marked the course of their lives together. "He taught me to see into the great visible world, and I taught him to see into the invisible world," she once remarked.

While they were sitting in the living room at Taliesin West just a few weeks before he died, Frank Lloyd Wright turned to his wife and said, "Mother, do you know who I wish would come here and have tea with us?"

She thought about their various friends across the decades and finally said, "No, who would you like me to invite?"

"William Blake. And I would sit at his feet to worship him. Such a wonderful man! He would understand us, Olgivanna. There would be a remarkable bond between the three of us just as there has been between you and me. And it occurred to me recently that in the distant future when they think of us, they will think of us as one. We blend, Olgivanna. We *are* one."

# APPENDIX A
## Sources of Quotations From Frank Lloyd Wright

Sources in brackets are keyed to the chronological list of Works Cited on the following page. Unpublished talks and letters are quoted from manuscripts in the archives of the Frank Lloyd Wright Foundation at Taliesin West. Numbers are page numbers.

*What Is Architecture? (pp. 7–8)*
First quotation, [1937]; second, [1908]; third, [1910]; fourth, [1936]; fifth, [1910]; sixth, [1954b].

*The Destruction of the Box (p. 9)*
First quotation, Olgivanna Lloyd Wright, *Frank Lloyd Wright: His Life, His Work, His Words* (1966); second, [1952a]; third, [1928g]; fourth, [1953a].

11, top, [1932]; 11, bottom, [1936]; 13, top, by hand on drawing, ca. 1950; 13, middle, inscription, Guggenheim Museum, 1960; 13, bottom, [1952b]; 15, top, [1950]; 15, bottom, [1957a]; 16, [1931b]; 19, top, [1931c]; 19, bottom, [1951a].

20, [1939]; 22, [1957a]; 24, all, [1957a]; 26, both, [1957a].

*The Nature of the Site (p. 28)*
First quotation, [1937]; second, [1957a].

28, [1932]; 30, [1940]; 31, [1931b]; 32, [1939]; 33, [1938]; 34, [1957a]; 35, all, [1957a]; 36, [1953b]; 37, [1937]; 38, both, [1943]; 39, on back of photo, ca. 1930.

40, [1957b]; 43, top, [1935]; 43, middle, to Edgar Kaufmann in conversation, 1935; 43, bottom, [1955a]; 44, both, [1938]; 46, [1910]; 47, [1910].

*Materials and Methods (p. 48)*
First quotation, [1930]; second, [1931b]; third, [1908]; fourth, [1931a].

48, [1928c]; 50, FLLW mss #2401.522, 1937; 51, [1928c]; 52, top, [1958a]; 52, bottom, [1910]; 53, [1902]; 54, [1928e]; 56, FLLW mss #2401.522, 1937; 58, [1928d]; 59, both, [1931b]; 60, both, [1931b].

62, top, [1951b]; 62, bottom, [1943]; 63, exhibition caption, 1930; 64, [1928f]; 66, top, [1928b]; 66, bottom, [1927b]; 67, top, by hand on drawing, 1954; 67, bottom, [1932]; 68, [1932]; 69, [1932]; 72, both, [1954a].

73, left, [1932]; 73, right, [1943]; 74, FLLW mss #2401.522, 1937; 75, both, by hand on drawing; 77, [1927a]; 79, [1957a]; 80, [1928a]; 81, [1943]; 82, left, [1939]; 82, right, [1927a]; 85, [1927a]; 86, by hand on drawing; 87, [1957a]; 88, both, [1957a].

*Building for Democracy (p. 89)*
First quotation, [1957a]; second, [1939]; third, [1957a]; fourth, Olgivanna Lloyd Wright, *Frank Lloyd Wright: His Life, His Work, His Words* (1966); fifth, [1957a]; sixth, [1954b].

90, [1945]; 91, [1945]; 92, left, [1945]; 92, right, [1955b]; 94, [1958b]; 95, top, [1958b]; 95, bottom, FLLW mss, ca. 1952; 97, top, [1948]; 97, bottom, FLLW mss, ca. 1952; 98, [1945].

99, [1958b]; 100, [1958b]; 101, [1945]; 102, [1958b]; 104, [1958b]; 105, [1945]; 106, [1948]; 107, [1958b]; 108, [1957a]; 110, [1958b]; 111, [1958b]; 112, [1958b]; 113, [1958b]; 114, [1945]; 115, [1945].

*In Conclusion (p. 116)*
First quotation, [1931a]; second, [1931c]; third, [1954b].

WORKS CITED

1902. Talk to the Chicago Women's Club
1908. *Architectural Record,* March
1910. *Sovereignty of the Individual.* Originally written and published as the text of *Ausgeführte Bauten und Entwürfe* (Berlin: Wasmuth).
1927a. *Architectural Record,* August
1927b. Idem, October
1928a. *Architectural Record,* January
1928b. Idem, February
1928c. Idem, April
1928d. Idem, May
1928e. Idem, June
1928f. Idem, August
1928g. Idem, December
1930. *Architectural Forum,* May
1931a. Talk to the Michigan Society of Architects, and Grand Rapids Chapter, American Institute of Architects
1931b. *Modern Architecture* (Princeton: Princeton University Press)
1931c. *Two Lectures on Architecture* (Chicago: Art Institute)
1932. *An Autobiography,* 1st ed. (New York: Longmans, Green)
1935. Letter to Robert Moses
1936. *Architect's Journal* (London), "Recollections. The United States: 1893–1920"
1937. *Architecture and Modern Life,* with Baker Brownell (New York: Harper and Brothers)
1938. Talk to the Association of Federal Architects
1939. *An Organic Architecture: The Architecture of Democracy* (London: Lund, Humphries)
1940. *Arizona Highways,* May
1943. *An Autobiography,* rev. ed. (New York: Duell, Sloan and Pearce)

1945. *When Democracy Builds* (Chicago: University of Chicago Press)
1948. *Architectural Forum,* January
1950. Talk to Taliesin Fellowship, May 28
1951a. *Architectural Forum,* January
1951b. Sixty Years of Living Architecture (exhibition)
1952a. Address to the Junior Chapter of the American Institute of Architects, New York City. Taped and typed: corrected by FLLW.
1952b. Talk to Taliesin Fellowship, August 13
1953a. *New York Times Magazine,* October 4
1953b. Letter to Signora Savina Masieri
1954a. *The Natural House* (New York: Horizon Press)
1954b. Talk to Taliesin Fellowship, October 10
1955a. Talk to Taliesin Fellowship, May 8
1955b. Letter to Lenkurt Electric Company
1957a. *A Testament* (New York: Horizon Press)
1957b. Address to Marin County on Presentation of Drawings for Civic Center
1958a. Talk to Taliesin Fellowship, December 14
1958b. *The Living City* (New York: Horizon Press)

# APPENDIX B
## Full Descriptions of Items Illustrated in Part I

Window. Darwin D. Martin Residence, 1904. Art glass, brass cames, oak frame. 41 × 25½ in. Darwin D. Martin House, School of Architecture and Design, State University of New York, Buffalo.

Barrel Chair. Herbert F. Johnson Residence ("Wingspread"), Windpoint, Wisconsin, 1937. Oak with upholstered seat. 30¼ × 19 × 20¾ in. The Johnson Foundation, Racine, Wisconsin.

59, top. "Cedar Rock," Lowell Walter House, Quasqueton, Iowa, 1945. Living room. © 1950 Ezra Stoller ESTO.

59, bottom. Drawing: Anderton Court Shops, Beverly Hills, California, 1952. Perspective detail. Copyright © The Frank Lloyd Wright Foundation 1968.

60. Administration Building for the S. C. Johnson and Son Co., Racine, Wisconsin, 1936. Interior detail of glass tubing. © Yukio Futagawa.

61. Beth Sholom Synagogue, Elkins Park, Pennsylvania, 1954. Interior. © Yukio Futagawa.

62, left. Drawing: "Romeo and Juliet" Windmill Tower for the Misses Lloyd-Jones, Hillside Home School, Spring Green, Wisconsin, 1896. Plan. Copyright © The Frank Lloyd Wright Foundation 1932.

62, right. "Romeo and Juliet" Windmill Tower. Courtesy the Frank Lloyd Wright Foundation.

63. Drawing: Project, Press Building for the *San Francisco Call*, San Francisco, 1912. Perspective. Copyright © The Frank Lloyd Wright Foundation 1942.

64. Drawing: Project, Rogers Lacy Hotel, Dallas, Texas, 1946. Perspective. Copyright © The Frank Lloyd Wright Foundation 1955.

65, top left. Drawing: Project, Rogers Lacy Hotel. Perspective detail of lobby. Copyright © The Frank Lloyd Wright Foundation 1982.

65, bottom left. Drawing: Project, Rogers Lacy Hotel. Plan of second floor. Copyright © The Frank Lloyd Wright Foundation 1988.

65, right. Drawing: Project, Rogers Lacy Hotel. Section. Copyright © The Frank Lloyd Wright Foundation 1987.

66, top. Drawing: Project, House for California, Los Angeles, 1921. Perspective. Copyright © The Frank Lloyd Wright Foundation 1962.

66, bottom. Drawing: Unity Temple, Oak Park, Illinois, 1904. Column detail and sketches. Copyright © The Frank Lloyd Wright Foundation 1959.

67, top. Drawing: Project, Harry Brown House, Genesco, Illinois, 1906. Perspective. Copyright © The Frank Lloyd Wright Foundation 1988.

67, bottom. Drawing: Isometric drawing of textile block system of construction, Los Angeles, 1921–24. Copyright © The Frank Lloyd Wright Foundation 1954.

68. "La Miniatura," Alice Millard House, Pasadena, California, 1923. © Yukio Futagawa.

69, top. John D. Storer House, Los Angeles, 1924. Living room. © Yukio Futagawa.

69, bottom. Drawing: Storer House. Ground floor and upper floor plans. Copyright © The Frank Lloyd Wright Foundation 1942.

70, top. Drawing: "How to Live in the Southwest," house for David Wright, Phoenix, Arizona, 1950. Conceptual plans, sections, and elevation. Copyright © The Frank Lloyd Wright Foundation 1976.

70, bottom. Drawing: David Wright House. Perspective. Copyright © The Frank Lloyd Wright Foundation 1976.

71. David Wright House. Photograph by P. E. Guerrero.

72, top. Toufic Kalil House, Manchester, New Hampshire, 1955. Living room. © Yukio Futagawa.

72, bottom. Drawing: Isometric drawing of the Usonian Automatic concrete block system of construction, 1950. Copyright © The Frank Lloyd Wright Foundation 1954.

73, left. Research Tower for the S. C. Johnson and Son Co., Racine, Wisconsin, 1944. Tower in construction. Photograph by S. C. Johnson and Son Co.

73, right. Administration Building for the S. C. Johnson and Son Co., Racine, Wisconsin, 1936. Detail of dendriform columns. © Yukio Futagawa.

74. Larkin Company Administration Building, Buffalo, New York, 1903. Steel desk and chair. (Shown in exhibition, Chicago.) Courtesy the Frank Lloyd Wright Foundation.

75, top. Drawing: Project, All-Steel Houses, Los Angeles, 1938. Conceptual section. Copyright © The Frank Lloyd Wright Foundation 1988.

75, bottom. Drawing: Project, All-Steel Houses. Plans, elevation, and view. Copyright © The Frank Lloyd Wright Foundation 1962.

Bookcase Doors. W. R. Heath Residence, Buffalo, New York, 1905. Art glass, zinc caming. 45¼ × 14⅛ in. Collection of The Frank Lloyd Wright Foundation.

Arm Chair. Frank Lloyd Wright Studio reception room, 1895. Oak with leather upholstery. 31½ × 25 × 25 in. Collection of Frank Lloyd Wright Foundation.

76. Anne Pfeiffer Chapel, Florida Southern College, Lakeland, Florida, 1938. Interior. © Yukio Futagawa.

77. Drawing: Anne Pfeiffer Chapel. Two plans and section. Copyright © The Frank Lloyd Wright Foundation 1942.

78. Guest house and covered walkway, "Fallingwater," Edgar J. Kaufmann House, Mill Run, Pennsylvania, 1938. View under guest house overhang. Photographed by Christopher Little.

79. Drawing: Project, Self-Service Garage for Edgar J. Kaufmann, Pittsburgh, 1949. Perspective detail. Copyright © The Frank Lloyd Wright Foundation 1962.

80, top. Drawing: Project, Steel and Glass Cathedral for William Norman Guthrie, New York, 1926. Conceptual elevation and notes. Copyright © The Frank Lloyd Wright Foundation 1955.

80, bottom. Drawing: Project, Steel and Glass Cathedral. Conceptual plan. Copyright © The Frank Lloyd Wright Foundation 1962.

81, top. Drawing: Project, "Century of Progress," pavilion for the Chicago World's Fair of 1933, Chicago, 1931. Copyright © The Frank Lloyd Wright Foundation 1985.

81, bottom. Drawing: Project, "Century of Progress." Schematic plan. Copyright © The Frank Lloyd Wright Foundation 1988.

82. Drawing: Project, Play Resort and Sports Club for Huntington Hartford, Hollywood, California, 1947. Perspective. Copyright © The Frank Lloyd Wright Foundation 1962.

83. Drawing: Project, Twin Cantilevered Bridges for The Pittsburgh Civic Center, Pittsburgh, 1948. Front elevation. Copyright © The Frank Lloyd Wright Foundation 1952.

84, top. Drawing: Project, Twin Cantilevered Bridges. Detail of stayed cables. Copyright © The Frank Lloyd Wright Foundation 1971.

84, bottom. Drawing: Project, Twin Cantilevered Bridges. Detail section of roadbeds. Copyright © The Frank Lloyd Wright Foundation 1988.

85. Drawing: Project, Twin Cantilevered Bridges. Night view. Copyright © The Frank Lloyd Wright Foundation 1952.

86. Drawing: Project, Mile High ILLINOIS, Chicago, 1956. Conceptual elevation, plan, and notes. Copyright © The Frank Lloyd Wright Foundation 1957.

87, left. Drawing: Project, Mile High ILLINOIS. Section and explanation. Copyright © The Frank Lloyd Wright Foundation 1957.

87, right. Drawing: Project, Mile High ILLINOIS. Perspective. Copyright © The Frank Lloyd Wright Foundation 1957.

88. Drawing: Project, Mile High ILLINOIS. Plan. Copyright © The Frank Lloyd Wright Foundation 1988.

BUILDING FOR DEMOCRACY

90. Drawing: Project, Broadacre City, 1934 (*The Living City*, 1958). Air view. Copyright © The Frank Lloyd Wright Foundation 1958.

91. Drawing: Project, Broadacre City. Air view. Copyright © The Frank Lloyd Wright Foundation 1962.

92. Drawing: Project, Lenkurt Electric Company Building, San Mateo, California, 1955. Perspective. Copyright © The Frank Lloyd Wright Foundation 1962.

93. Drawing: Project, Lenkurt Electric Company Building. View into patio-cafe. Copyright © The Frank Lloyd Wright Foundation 1985.

94, top. Project, The Unified Farm, 1931. Model.

94, bottom. Drawing: Project, The Unified Farm. Copyright © The Frank Lloyd Wright Foundation 1958.

95, top. Drawing: Project, Rosenwald School, La Jolla, California, 1928. Copyright © The Frank Lloyd Wright Foundation 1955.

95, bottom. Drawing: Florida Southern College, Lakeland, Florida, 1938. Perspective. Copyright © The Frank Lloyd Wright Foundation 1942.

96. Florida Southern College. Esplanade. © Yukio Futagawa.

97, top. Roux Library, Florida Southern College, 1941. Reading room. © Yukio Futagawa.

97, bottom. Roux Library, Florida Southern College. © Yukio Futagawa.

98. Theodore Baird House, Amherst, Massachusetts, 1940. © Yukio Futagawa.

99. Drawing: Project, Christian Science Church, Bolinas, California, 1956. Perspective. Copyright © The Frank Lloyd Wright Foundation 1957.

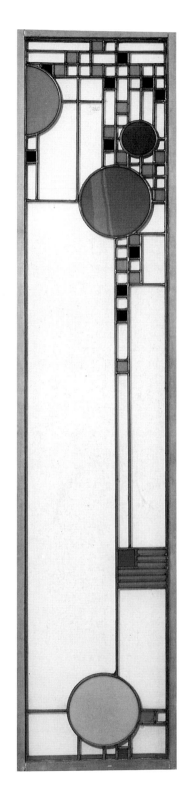

Window (Composition in Light). Avery Coonley Playhouse, Riverside, Illinois. Art glass, lead caming, painted wood frame. 60½ × 12 in. Walter and Dawn Clark Netsch Collection, courtesy of Miami University Art Museum, Oxford, Ohio.

Side Chair. Clarence Sondern Residence, Kansas City, Missouri, 1940.
Cypress plywood with upholstery. 27⅛ × 21½ × 22⅞ in. Domino's Pizza
Collection.

100, top. Drawing: Dallas Theatre Center, Dallas, Texas, 1955. Perspective. Copyright © The Frank Lloyd Wright Foundation 1962.

100, bottom. Drawing: Dallas Theatre Center. Plan. Copyright © The Frank Lloyd Wright Foundation 1958.

101, top. Isador Zimmerman House, Manchester, New Hampshire, 1950. © Ezra Stoller Esto 1952.

101, bottom. Drawing: Zimmerman House. Plan. Copyright © The Frank Lloyd Wright Foundation 1988.

102, top. Drawing: Project, Crystal Heights, hotel, apartments, shops, theater, and parking, Washington, D.C., 1939. Perspective. Copyright © The Frank Lloyd Wright Foundation 1942.

102, bottom. Drawing: Project, Crystal Heights. Ground plan. Copyright © The Frank Lloyd Wright Foundation 1986.

103, top. Drawing: Project, Crystal Heights. Typical tower plan. Copyright © The Frank Lloyd Wright Foundation 1942.

103, bottom. Drawing: Project, Crystal Heights. Conceptual elevation. Copyright © The Frank Lloyd Wright Foundation 1962.

104, top. Drawing: Project, "Cloverleaf," quadruple housing, Pittsfield, Massachusetts, 1942. Perspective. Copyright © The Frank Lloyd Wright Foundation 1969.

104, bottom. Drawing: Project, "Cloverleaf." Plan. Copyright © The Frank Lloyd Wright Foundation 1954.

105. Drawing: Project, "Golden Beacon," office tower and apartments, Chicago, 1956. Perspective. Copyright © The Frank Lloyd Wright Foundation 1959.

106. Drawing: Project, "Butterfly Bridge" for the Wisconsin River, 1947. Perspective. Copyright © The Frank Lloyd Wright Foundation 1962.

107. Drawing: Project, Marin County Fair Pavilion, San Rafael, California, 1957–59. Interior perspective. Copyright © The Frank Lloyd Wright Foundation 1959.

108, top. Drawing: Project, "Oasis," Arizona State Capitol, Phoenix, 1957. Air view. Copyright © The Frank Lloyd Wright Foundation 1957.

Work Station. S. C. Johnson Administration Building, Racine, Wisconsin, 1936–39. Painted steel and walnut, with upholstery: desk 33¾ × 84 × 32 in.; chair 36 × 17¾ × 20 in. S. C. Johnson & Son, courtesy of Milwaukee Art Museum.

108, bottom. Drawing: Project, "Oasis," Arizona State Capitol. View along colonnade into court. Copyright © The Frank Lloyd Wright Foundation 1959.

109, top. Drawing: Project, "Oasis," Arizona State Capitol. Ground floor plan. Copyright © The Frank Lloyd Wright Foundation 1957.

109, bottom. Drawing: Project, "Oasis," Arizona State Capitol. Section. Copyright © The Frank Lloyd Wright Foundation 1957.

110. Drawing: Project, Pittsburgh Point Park Civic Center, Pittsburgh, 1947. Perspective. Copyright © The Frank Lloyd Wright Foundation 1962.

111, top. Drawing: Project, Pittsburgh Point Park Civic Center. Detail section. Copyright © The Frank Lloyd Wright Foundation 1962.

111, bottom. Drawing: Project, Pittsburgh Point Park Civic Center. Cross section. Copyright © The Frank Lloyd Wright Foundation 1962.

112. Sidney Bazett House, Hillsborough, California, 1940. Interior.

113. Drawing: Project, Motel for Daniel Wieland, Hagerstown, Maryland, 1956. Perspective. Copyright © The Frank Lloyd Wright Foundation 1958.

114. Drawing: Gerald Tonkens House, Amberley Village, Ohio, 1954. Perspective. Copyright © The Frank Lloyd Wright Foundation 1976.

115. Drawing: Project, Gerald Sussman House, Poundridge, New York, 1955. Perspective. Copyright © The Frank Lloyd Wright Foundation 1985.

# SELECTED BIBLIOGRAPHY

PRIMARY SOURCES

*Books*

*Ausgeführte Bauten und Entwürfe von Frank Lloyd Wright*. Berlin: Verlag Ernst Wasmuth A.G., 1910. Reprints. *Buildings, Plans and Designs*. New York: Horizon Press, 1963. *Studies and Executed Buildings*. New York: Rizzoli, 1986.

*An Autobiography*. London: Longmans, Green, 1932. Rev. ed. New York: Duell, Sloan and Pearce, 1943. Reprint. New York: Horizon Press, 1977.

*The Disappearing City*. New York: William Farquhar Payson, 1932. Rev. ed. *The Industrial Revolution Runs Away*. New York: Horizon Press, 1969.

With Baker Brownell. *Architecture and Modern Life*. New York: Harper and Brothers, 1937.

*Frank Lloyd Wright on Architecture: Selected Writings, 1894–1940*. Edited and with an introduction by Frederick Gutheim. New York: Duell, Sloan and Pearce, 1940.

*When Democracy Builds*. Chicago: University of Chicago Press, 1945.

*Genius and the Mobocracy*. New York: Duell, Sloan and Pearce, 1949. Rev. ed. New York: Horizon Press, 1971.

*The Future of Architecture*. New York: Horizon Press, 1953.

*An American Architecture*. Edited by Edgar Kaufmann, Jr. New York: Horizon Press, 1955.

*The Story of the Tower: The Tree That Escaped the Crowded Forest*. New York: Horizon Press, 1956.

*A Testament*. New York: Horizon Press, 1957.

*The Living City*. New York: Horizon Press, 1958.

*Frank Lloyd Wright: Writings and Buildings*. Selected by Edgar Kaufmann, Jr., and Ben Raeburn. New York: Horizon Press, 1960.

*Frank Lloyd Wright: The Early Work*. New York: Horizon Press, 1968.

*The Industrial Revolution Runs Away*. New York: Horizon Press, 1969.

*In the Cause of Architecture, Frank Lloyd Wright: With a Symposium on Architecture with and without Wright by Eight Who Knew Him*. Edited by Frederick Gutheim, containing Wright's essays for the *Architectural Record*. New York: Architectural Record Books, 1975.

*Collected Lectures*

*Modern Architecture: Being the Kahn Lectures for 1930*. Princeton: Princeton University Press, 1931. Reprint. Carbondale: Southern Illinois University Press, 1987.

*Two Lectures on Architecture*. Chicago: Art Institute, 1931.

*An Organic Architecture: The Architecture of Democracy*. London: Lund Humphries, 1939.

*Frank Lloyd Wright: His Living Voice*. Edited and with commentary by Bruce Brooks Pfeiffer. Fresno: The Press at California State University, 1987.

*Correspondence*

*Letters to Apprentices*. Selected and with commentary by Bruce Brooks Pfeiffer. Fresno: The Press at California State University, 1982.

*Letters to Architects.* Selected and with commentary by Bruce Brooks Pfeiffer. Fresno: The Press at California State University, 1984.

*Letters to Clients.* Selected and with commentary by Bruce Brooks Pfeiffer. Fresno: The Press at California State University, 1986.

*Frank Lloyd Wright: The Guggenheim Correspondence.* Selected and with commentary by Bruce Brooks Pfeiffer. Fresno: The Press at California State University; Carbondale: Southern Illinois University Press, 1986.

*Studies, Designs, Drawings, Executed Projects*

*Taliesin Drawings: Recent Architecture of Frank Lloyd Wright Selected from His Drawings.* New York: Wittenborn, Schultz, 1952.

*The Drawings of Frank Lloyd Wright.* Selected by Arthur Drexler. New York: Horizon Press for the Museum of Modern Art, 1962.

*Frank Lloyd Wright: Johnson & Son, Administration Building and Research Tower, Racine, Wisconsin, 1936–9.* Edited by Yukio Futagawa. The Series of Global Architecture, no. 1. Tokyo: A. D. A. Edita, 1970.

*Frank Lloyd Wright: Kaufmann House, "Fallingwater," Bear Run, Pennsylvania, 1936.* Edited by Yukio Futagawa. The Series of Global Architecture, no. 2. Tokyo: A. D. A. Edita, 1970.

*Frank Lloyd Wright: Taliesin East, Spring Green, Wisconsin, 1925– ; Taliesin West, Paradise Valley, Arizona, 1938– .* Edited by Yukio Futagawa. The Series of Global Architecture, no. 15. Tokyo: A. D. A. Edita, 1972.

*Frank Lloyd Wright: Houses in Oak Park and River Forest, Illinois, 1889–1913.* Edited by Yukio Futagawa. The Series of Global Architecture, no. 25. Tokyo: A. D. A. Edita, 1973.

*Frank Lloyd Wright: Solomon R. Guggenheim Museum, New York City, N.Y., 1943–59; Marin County Civic Center, California, 1957–1970.* Edited by Yukio Futagawa. Global Architecture Series, no. 36. Tokyo: A. D. A. Edita, 1975.

*Houses by Frank Lloyd Wright 1.* Edited by Yukio Futagawa. Global Interiors, no. 9. Tokyo: A. D. A. Edita, 1975.

*Frank Lloyd Wright: Pfeiffer Chapel, Florida Southern College, Lakeland, Florida, 1938; Beth Sholom Synagogue, Elkins Park,* *Pennsylvania, 1954.* Edited by Yukio Futagawa. Global Architecture, no. 40. Tokyo: A. D. A. Edita, 1976.

*Houses by Frank Lloyd Wright 2.* Edited by Yukio Futagawa. Global Interiors, no. 10. Tokyo: A. D. A. Edita, 1976.

*The Imperial Hotel, Tokyo, Japan, 1915–22.* Edited by Yukio Futagawa. Global Architecture, no. 53. Tokyo: A. D. A. Edita, 1980.

*Frank Lloyd Wright.* Edited by Bruce Brooks Pfeiffer. 7 vols. to date. Tokyo: A. D. A. Edita, 1984– .

*Treasures of Taliesin: 76 Unbuilt Designs of Frank Lloyd Wright.* Edited by Bruce Brooks Pfeiffer. Fresno: The Press at California State University; Carbondale: Southern Illinois University Press, 1986.

SECONDARY SOURCES

Brooks, H. Allen. *The Prairie School: Frank Lloyd Wright and His Midwest Contemporaries.* Toronto: University of Toronto Press, 1972.

Brownell, Baker, and Frank Lloyd Wright. *Architecture and Modern Life.* New York: Harper and Brothers, 1937.

Eaton, Leonard K. *Two Chicago Architects and Their Clients: Frank Lloyd Wright and Howard Van Doren Shaw.* Cambridge: MIT Press, 1969.

Farr, Finis. *Frank Lloyd Wright: A Biography.* New York: Charles Scribner's Sons, 1961.

Fries, H. de, ed. *Frank Lloyd Wright: Aus dem Lebenswerke eines Architekten.* Berlin: Verlag Ernst Pollak, 1926.

Hanks, David A. *The Decorative Designs of Frank Lloyd Wright.* New York: Dutton, 1979.

Hanna, Paul R., and Jean S. Hanna. *Frank Lloyd Wright's Hanna House: The Clients' Report.* Cambridge: Architectural History Foundation and MIT Press, 1981. Reprint. Carbondale: Southern Illinois University Press, 1987.

Hitchcock, Henry-Russell. *In the Nature of Materials, 1887–1941, The Buildings of Frank Lloyd Wright.* New York: Duell, Sloan and Pearce, 1942. Rev. ed. New York: Da Capo, 1973.

Hoffman, Donald. *Frank Lloyd Wright's Fallingwater: The House and Its History*. New York: Dover, 1978.

———. *Frank Lloyd Wright's Robie House: The Illustrated Story of an Architectural Masterpiece*. New York: Dover, 1984.

Izzo, Alberto, and Camillo Gubitosi. *Frank Lloyd Wright: Disegni, 1887–1959*. Florence: Centro Di, 1976.

Jacobs, Herbert, and Katherine Jacobs. *Building with Frank Lloyd Wright: An Illustrated Memoir*. San Francisco: Chronicle Books, 1978. Reprint. Carbondale: Southern Illinois University Press, 1986.

Jencks, Charles. *Kings of Infinite Space: Frank Lloyd Wright and Michael Graves*. Based on a BBC film by Charles Jencks. London: Academy Editions, 1983.

Kaufmann, Edgar, Jr. *Fallingwater: A Frank Lloyd Wright Country House*. New York: Abbeville Press, 1986.

———. "Frank Lloyd Wright at the Metropolitan Museum of Art." *Metropolitan Museum of Art Bulletin* 40 (Fall 1982), pp. 1–48.

Lipman, Jonathan. *Frank Lloyd Wright and the Johnson Wax Buildings*. New York: Rizzoli, 1986.

Manson, Grant Carpenter. *Frank Lloyd Wright to 1910: The First Golden Age*. New York: Reinhold, 1958.

Meehan, Patrick. *The Master Architect: Conversations with Frank Lloyd Wright*. New York: John Wiley and Sons, 1984.

Pappas, Bette K. *Frank Lloyd Wright: No Passing Fancy, A Pictorial History*. St. Louis: privately printed, 1985.

Pawley, Martin, and Yukio Futagawa. *Frank Lloyd Wright, I: Public Buildings*. New York: Simon and Schuster, 1970.

Preston, Charles, and Edward A. Hamilton, eds. "Frank Lloyd Wright." In *Mike Wallace Asks: Highlights from Forty-six Controversial Interviews*. New York: Simon and Schuster, 1958.

Scully, Vincent, Jr. *Frank Lloyd Wright*. New York: George Braziller, 1960.

Sergeant, John. *Frank Lloyd Wright's Usonian Houses: The Case for Organic Architecture*. New York: Whitney Library of Design, 1976.

Storrer, William Allin. *The Architecture of Frank Lloyd Wright: A Complete Catalogue*. Cambridge: MIT Press, 1974.

Sweeney, Robert L. *Frank Lloyd Wright: An Annotated Bibliography*. Los Angeles: Hennessey and Ingalls, 1978.

Tafel, Edgar. *Apprentice to Genius: Years with Frank Lloyd Wright*. New York: McGraw-Hill, 1979.

Twombly, Robert C. *Frank Lloyd Wright: An Interpretive Biography*. New York: Harper and Row, 1973.

———. *Frank Lloyd Wright: His Life and His Architecture*. New York: Wiley, 1979.

Wijdeveld, H. Th., ed. *The Life-Work of the American Architect Frank Lloyd Wright*. Santpoort, Holland: C. A. Mees, 1925. Rev. ed. New York: Horizon Press, 1965.

Wright, Iovanna Lloyd. *Architecture: Man in Possession of His Earth*. Edited by Patricia Coyle Nicholson. Garden City, N.Y.: Doubleday, 1962.

Wright, Olgivanna Lloyd. *Our House*. New York: Horizon Press, 1959.

———. *The Shining Brow: Frank Lloyd Wright*. New York: Horizon Press, 1960.

———. *The Roots of Life*. New York: Horizon Press, 1963.

———. *Frank Lloyd Wright: His Life, His Work, His Words*. New York: Horizon Press, 1966.